Nairne's Muskhogean Journals

From the collections of the Henry E. Huntington Library and Art Gallery, San Marino, California. Published with permission.

Nairne's Muskhogean Journals
The 1708 Expedition
to the Mississippi River

EDITED, WITH AN INTRODUCTION, BY
Alexander Moore

UNIVERSITY PRESS OF MISSISSIPPI
Jackson and London

Library of Congress Cataloging-in-Publication Data

Nairne, Thomas, d. 1715.
  [Journalls to the Chicasaws and Talapoosies]
  Nairne's Muskhogean journals: the 1708 expedition to the Mississippi
River / edited, with an introduction by Alexander Moore.
    p.   cm.
  Bibliography: p.
  Includes index.
  ISBN 0-87805-346-8 (alk. paper)
  1. Muskhogean Indians—History—Sources. 2. Chickasaw Indians—
History—Sources. 3. South Carolina—History—Colonial period,
1600-1775—Sources. I. Moore, Alexander, 1948-   . II. Title.
III. Title: Journalls to the Chicasaws and Talapoosies.
E99.M95N34 1988
975.5'00497—dc19
                          87-27683
                            CIP

Contents

Foreword

For many years historians and anthropologists have praised the insights of Thomas Nairne into the lifeways of Southeastern Indians. Their admiration and his presumed insights were based upon a single document, a memorial he wrote in 1708 embodying his recommendations as Indian Agent of South Carolina. It was not known that his memorial was only one of five letters written that year, and not the most important for history or anthropology. The finding of the four letters that constitute Nairne's *Journalls to the Chicasaws and Talapoosies*, which have been safely if obscurely ensconced in the British Library since 1931, is another example of the familiar serendipity of historical scholarship. While researching another topic from another era, Alexander Moore encountered the letters and immediately recognized both their importance and the fact that they had not been used by scholars. He undertook to prepare the edition presented here. The contribution that this material can make to scholarship in many areas is inestimable. In addition, Moore has provided us with the historical context that enables us to evaluate Nairne's contributions.

Nairne himself was a fascinating character whose life and experiences placed him in a unique position both to observe and to understand the social institutions of Southeastern Indians at the turn of the eighteenth century. Although he certainly had a strategy to argue with respect to those Indians, comparison of the letters of the *Journalls* with the more familiar memorial (printed here as an appendix to bring all five letters together) shows that he ground most of his axes of imperial strategy in the latter. He accorded his friends and fellow participants in the Indian trade, Thomas Smith, Ralph Izard, and Robert Fenwick, a more detailed account of his observations and personal experiences among the

Southeastern Indians. Certainly Nairne suffered from the normal dose of ethnocentrism, but his employment of comparisons to classical and Biblical models as tools for discerning differences as well as parallels—so different from James Adair's strained efforts to prove the Indians part of the Lost Tribes of Israel—shows that he did recognize the Indians' uniqueness in the world and was prepared to understand the workings of their institutions on their own terms. In his curiosity lies the value of his observations.

The historian of white colonial America will find in these letters the foundations of Nairne's grand strategy of imperial domination of the Southeast—even to legalistic arguments about primacy of contact with Indian groups. Nairne's force of character and his credibility as an Indian Agent made his strategy that of Carolina's for the early years of the eighteenth century. That he seriously overestimated the Indians' tolerance for externally-directed intertribal conflict became apparent in the Yemassee War of 1715. The Carolinians' imperialist activities precipitated a rebellion against the English all across the Southeast and enabled the French regime in Louisiana to entrench itself literally in forts deep in Indian country. Perhaps there was justice rather than irony in the fact that Nairne was the first victim of the war. Although his appreciation of Indian lifeways showed a degree of humane understanding, the use to which he and other Carolinians put his knowledge constituted a betrayal of humane ideals remarkable even by the standards of his time.

The anthropologist whose interest centers on the Muskogean cultural groups of the Southeast will be literally astounded by the detail to be found in these letters. Nairne was particularly interested in sociopolitical organization and its process. Because his pragmatic obsession was the management of Indian groups, he was concerned especially to learn where the springs of power and influence lay among the Indians and the conventions by which influence was exercised. It is interesting to observe what he wrote to what correspondent, for clearly he divided his themes. To Robert Fenwick he wrote of the methods and plenty of the hunt and about French rivalry for the favor of the Chickasaws. Thomas Smith received a study of the governance of the Talapoosas and Ocheses. Ralph Izard learned a wealth of details on Indian institutions and character. Indeed, Nairne wrote to Izard more and in greater detail upon Chickasaw institutions than their self-proclaimed champion James Adair provided in a whole book. He also sent to Izard insightful speculations on the evolution of the historic Southeastern tribes— more insightful than many relatively modern anthropologists have been able to muster. The information he sent Izard on the *Fani Mingo* institution literally explains the function of the calumet ceremony in the Southeast as it has not been understood heretofore. His description of the initiation of a young man into the warrior class may provide insight into the significance of the so-called "bilobed arrow" depicted in the hair of dancing figures that are part of late Mississippian iconography. Lastly, his explanation of the process of "daughter village" formation and its mechanism in exogamous clans will henceforth be offered to students of anthropology as a clear confirmation of theory.

I think Nairne's self-interest and that of his correspondents assured that his attempt at accuracy was sincere and there are good reasons to believe that the goal of accuracy was largely achieved. More detailed study will be required to determine precisely which of the details Narine described were personally observed by him and which depended upon oral testimony, either from English traders or the Indians themselves. Until that study is complete we cannot take every statement completely as read; but, within those limitations, the value of these remarkable letters is obvious. Moore has laid the foundation by providing the scholar with a text that can be trusted to replace the original for most purposes. He has also given the details of manuscript transmission that enable us to evaluate the relationship between the original letters and the documentary *Journall* in which they survive. I can only add that I am delighted that this work is being given the exposure it needs in order to elicit the further study it deserves.

Patricia Galloway

Mississippi Department of Archives and History
Jackson

Acknowledgments

"Capt. Thomas Nairne's Journalls to the Chicasaws and Talapoosies" is owned by the Department of Manuscripts, British Library, London, and Nairne's memorial of 10 July 1708 is among the state papers of the Great Britain Public Record Office, London. The liberal publication policies of these two institutions make possible this work. The British Public Record Office also owns and has granted permission to publish Richard Beresford's map of the Southeast, ca. 1715. The equally liberal policy of the Geography and Map Division of the Library of Congress, Washington, D.C., permits reproduction of Herman Moll's "New Map of the North Parts of America Claimed by France, 1720." I wish to acknowledge the permission granted by the Henry E. Huntington Library and Art Gallery, San Marino, California, to publish Thomas Nairne's "A Map of South Carolina [1711]" and to quote from the Huntington Library's collection of Nairne manuscripts. A Summer Research Fellowship at the John Carter Brown Library, Providence, R.I., in June 1986 allowed me to revise the annotations and introduction in the cordial and multi-talented company of the staff of that institution. Three individuals have made important contributions to this work. They are James R. Atkinson, Archaeologist, National Park Service, Natchez Trace Parkway, Tupelo, Miss.; Professor Walter B. Edgar, Director, Institute for Southern Studies, University of South Carolina, Columbia; and Patricia Galloway, Special Projects Director, Mississippi Department of Archives and History, Jackson. Dr. Galloway's insightful foreword is only the most visible of her contributions to this project. She has provided me with information and encouragement in equal measures for the last three years. Ms. Elizabeth Dozier, Staff Assistant of the University of South Carolina Institute for Southern Studies, assisted in preparing the index.

Nairne's Muskhogean Journals

Introduction

Thomas Nairne was a notable figure in the history of Proprietary South Carolina. Author of Carolina's Indian policy and an
enlightened political leader in the Commons House of Assembly,
he deeply impressed his ideas and character upon the province
in the early decades of the eighteenth century.[1] Nairne was a soldier
and diplomat among the Indians of the Southeast and an early
chronicler of their customs and ceremonies. His *A Letter from
South-Carolina*, published in 1710, was a perceptive analysis of
Carolina society and a tract to encourage immigration there.[2]
Despite these accomplishments, Nairne is known today primarily
for only two reasons, his authorship of a memorial to Charles
Spencer, Earl of Sunderland, on British imperial strategy in the
Southeast, and for his spectacular death by torture at the hands
of the Yemassee Indians in 1715.

For students of Southern history, Thomas Nairne's memorial
of July 10, 1708, to the Earl of Sunderland, is of signal importance.
Verner W. Crane, the foremost historian of the southern colonial
frontier, described it as "one of the most remarkable documents
in the history of Anglo-American imperialism." In his memorial
Nairne outlined a bold plan for the British to use the fur, deerskin, and Indian slave trade to take control of the whole mid-
continent of North America. With these economic weapons he
sought to gain the allegiance of powerful Indian tribes throughout
the Mississippi River Valley, from the Gulf of Mexico to the Great
Lakes. He then planned to direct this British-Indian alliance against
the French and Spanish colonies in North America.

Nairne's memorial sprang partly from his powerful imagina-
tion but was also the product of first-hand experience. In January
1708 Nairne and Thomas Welch, a Carolina trader among the
Chickasaw Indians, traveled from Charles Town to the banks of

3

the Mississippi River on a diplomatic mission to the Southeastern Indian tribes. Nairne wrote a series of letters to the Board of Commissioners of the Indian Trade in Charles Town datelined from the towns he and Welch visited. Four of these letters, transcribed, bound together, and titled "Capt. Thomas Nairne's Journalls to the Chicasaws and Talapoosies," recorded the events of the expedition as they occurred. In addition, Nairne's *Journalls* contained the earliest and fullest ethnographical accounts extant in English of the Ochese, Talapoosa, and Chickasaw Indians.[3]

To complement his *Journalls* and memorial, Nairne drew a map of the Southeast, which he also sent to the Earl of Sunderland. Although his original map has been lost, an abridged version of it was published in London in 1711 as an inset to Edward Crisp's "A Compleat Description of the Province of Carolina in 3 Parts." Entitled "A Map of South Carolina Shewing the Settlements of the English, French & Indian Nations from Charles Town to the River Mississipi," Nairne's inset marked the route of his expedition, the locations and populations of the tribes he and Welch visited, and a rough outline of English territorial claims in the Southeast (frontis). Nairne also contributed another inset to Crisp's "Map of Carolina." This second one, entitled "A New Chart of the Coast of Carolina and Florida from Cape Henry to the Havana in the Island of Cuba," was, according to the map legend, composed by "Cap. Tho. Nairn and others." It retained the same coastal features of Nairne's more famous inset, including the depiction of Florida as an archipelago, but lacked the other inset's diplomatic and political significance.[4] The London mapmaker Herman Moll quickly incorporated Nairne's maps into his own work. In 1715 he published "A New and Exact Map of the Dominions of the King of Great Britain on the Continent of North America" and in 1720 "A New Map of the North Parts of America Claimed by France" (map 2). Both included features from Nairne's insets (possibly from his original manuscript maps) as well as information derived from Nairne's *Journalls*.[5]

Although Nairne and the British failed in the short run to accomplish his imperial scheme, his plans were ultimately realized

Nairne's Route and Itinerary

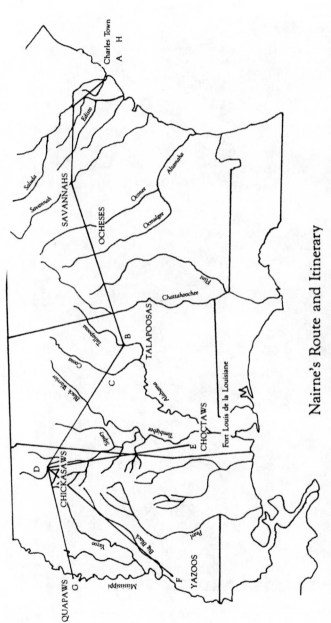

A. November 28, 1707. At Charles Town. *Journal of the Commons House of Assembly . October 22, 1707–February 12, 1707/8*, pp. 56–57.

B. January 20, 1708. At "Ogfaskee," the chief town of the upper Talapoosas. The town is located on Nairne's inset and on John Mitchell's "A Map of the British and French Dominions in North America, 1755," on the present-day Tallapoosa River. Frontispiece and William P. Cumming, *The Southeast in Early Maps* (revised ed., Chapel Hill: University of North Carolina Press, 1962), plate 59.

C. February 25, 1708. Crossed the "Cusa" or Coosa River.

D. April 12, 13, 15, 1708. Among the Chickasaws at "Hollachatroe," commonly called Falatchao. Swanton, "Social and Religious Beliefs and Usages of the Chickasaw Indians," ... ... south of the Chickasaw tribes. Nairne's ... ... ted on his map

(see frontispiece) and is labeled "Course of Capt. Nairn's Journey" on John Barnwell's manuscript map of the Southeast, *ca.* 1722. Cumming, *Southeast in Early Maps*, plate 48.

F. *Ca.* May, 1708. Thomas Welch visited the Yazoo and other lower Mississippi tribes. Petition of Thomas Welch, December 9, 1708, in *Journal of the Commons House of Assembly*, November 24, 1708–November 5, 1709, ms. volume at Sc-Ar.

G. Approximate site of Thomas Welch's trading station among the Quapaw Indians, *ca.* 1698. The route to Welch's station is marked on frontispiece. See also W. David Baird, *The Quapaw Indians. A History of the Downstream People* (Norman: University of Oklahoma Press, 1980), pp. 27–29.

H. June 24, 1708. Nairne at Charles Town. Nathaniel Johnson to John Collins, June 24, 1708, mittimus committing Nairne to jail. Huntington Ms. 22269, Henry E. Huntington Library and Art Gallery, San Marino, Ca.

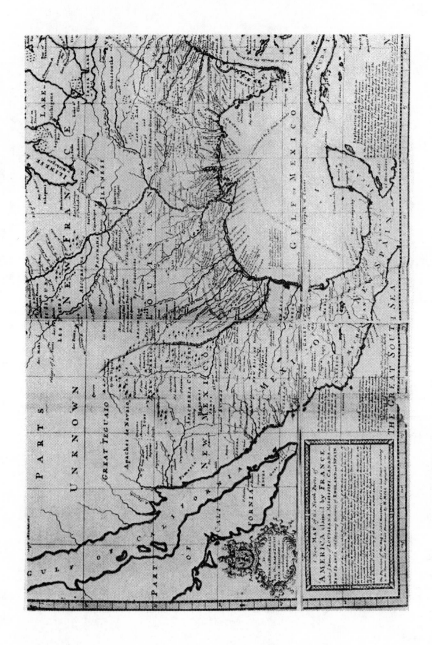

Map 2

From the Map Division, Library of Congress. Published with permission.

by the youthful United States of America. Although he was murdered by Indians his *Journalls* preserved information on Indian ethnology that outlasted the tribes themselves. His *Journalls*, memorial, and maps guided Carolina and British officials in the formation of policy throughout the eighteenth century. They also recorded and preserved the events of a Carolina expedition that rivaled the far-flung exploits of the Spanish *conquistadores* and French *coureurs de bois*.

It is fortunate that Thomas Nairne's place in South Carolina history rests upon his public career and not upon his private life. His career is well documented in the public records of the province while information on his private life is sketchy. Nairne was a native Scot and his surname suggested family connections with Nairne, in northeastern Scotland, but the place and date of his birth are unknown.[6] His earliest recorded presence in Carolina is January 1695, when he witnessed the will of Richard Quintyne, a Berkeley County planter.[7] Nairne must have been at least twenty-one years of age in 1695 to have acted as a legal witness, but he was probably several years older. He may have emigrated directly from Scotland to Carolina but his early acquaintance with Quintyne, a Londoner transplanted to Carolina via Barbados, suggests that he may have had Barbadian connections.

Shortly after Richard Quintyne's death Nairne married his widow, Elizabeth Edward Quintyne, herself a native Scot born in 1658. Elizabeth Nairne had four children from her marriage to Quintyne, Jane, Elizabeth, Henry, and Mary, and a stepdaughter Martha Quintyne. Henry Quintyne died in August 1716, killed, like his stepfather Nairne, during the Yemassee War. Mary Quintyne married William Bull, later lieutenant governor of South Carolina.[8] In addition to her children, Elizabeth Nairne brought to her marriage landholdings in Berkeley County which Nairne augmented by land grants from the Lords Proprietors. He concentrated his acquisitions on Saint Helena Island, south of Charles Town, where he accumulated nearly 3,600 acres and resided "among the Indians."[9] Thomas and Elizabeth Nairne had only one son, Thomas, born in 1698. Thomas Jr. died in 1718 and the surname vanished from South Carolina history.[10]

In *A Letter from South-Carolina* Nairne stated that he had exchanged "the unhappy Condition of the Military Imployment" for the life of a Carolina planter. He defined planters as that class of Carolinians who lived "by their own and their Servants' Industry, improve their Estates, follow Tillage or Grasing, and make those Commodities which are transported from hence to Great Britain, and other places."[11] In accordance with this self-description Nairne probably grew rice, provisions, or indigo. But planting was not his sole source of livelihood. He surveyed land for his neighbors and at least once actively engaged in the Indian slave trade. Herman Moll's "A New Map of the North Parts of America Claimed by France" recorded an expedition by Nairne and thirty-three Yemassee Indians into Florida to capture slaves. The expedition took place in 1702 and penetrated as far as the Everglades region of Florida. Nairne and his Yemassee henchmen captured thirty-five Florida Indians, brought them back to Charles Town, and sold them as slaves.[12] He also earned income from public offices. At various times Nairne was a magistrate, militia captain, admiralty judge, and provincial Indian Agent. In this last office he had an annual salary of £250, a sum which compared favorably with the governor's £200 per year.[13]

Neither a will nor an inventory of Nairne's estate has been found. Surprised by death he may not have left a will. The Yemassee War halted virtually all legal processes in Carolina for two years and made it unlikely that his estate was inventoried. At any rate, given the destruction in Colleton and Granville counties by the Indians, it is likely that little or nothing remained of Nairne's plantation to inventory. An inventory of the estate of Nairne's widow, who died on March 9, 1721, at sixty years of age, is among the public records of South Carolina. Her estate was appraised at a total value of £3,669.10 Carolina money. Twenty-seven slaves, including five Indians, accounted for £2,690 of this amount.[14] With her husband and son dead and her plantation ruined, Elizabeth Nairne did not remarry and probably accumulated little land or capital during her last years. Her wealth in 1721 likely reflected what remained of Thomas Nairne's estate after 1715.

Although Nairne claimed in *A Letter from South-Carolina* to have forsaken the military profession, in truth he was a soldier all his life. He commanded Indian and white troops in 1702 at the siege of St. Augustine and again in 1704 against the Apalachee Indians. Indeed, even his 1702 slave-catching raid was a military operation as well as an economic venture. Nairne was also a soldier off the battlefield. As a member of the South Carolina Commons House of Assembly he was often involved in military matters. In 1707 he was a member of Commons House committees to inspect provincial gunpowder stores and to inspect the fortifications at Charles Town. He also helped to organize a lookout and scout boat system to provide warning of Indian and Spanish raids along the frontier. His plantation on St. Helena was fortified and mounted with cannon to serve as the southernmost link in a chain of plantation forts along the seacoast. Nairne did not command troops during the Tuscarora War in North Carolina but authored legislation that sent a relief expedition there in 1712.[15] Of course the best evidence of Nairne's military activities is found in his *Journalls* and memorial to Sunderland. He understood Indian warfare and sought through diplomacy to combine intertribal conflict and slaving raids with the imperial aspirations of British Carolinians.

Thomas Nairne first entered the Commons House in January 1706 to represent Colleton County.[16] This was the first Assembly elected under the provisions of "An Act for the More Effectual Preservation of the Government. . . ." Commonly called the Exclusion Act, this law was passed in May 1704 by an Assembly rigidly controlled by Governor Nathaniel Johnson and his "High Church" party. It required that all persons elected to the Commons House take Holy Communion in the Church of England before claiming their seats. If members refused to conform, they had to swear publicly that they had not communicated in the church of any other denomination within a year. At a later session, the same Assembly enacted "An Act for the Establishment of Religious Worship according to the Church of England," which made Anglicanism the officially established religion of the province.[17]

The religious character of these two statutes was important but so was their political aspect. Using them, Governor Johnson hoped to bar his political opponents, most of whom were Dissenters, from the Commons House by forcing them to choose between membership and religious apostasy. Most of his opponents lived in Nairne's region, Colleton County, while his supporters resided in Berkeley County. The Exclusion Act effectually barred Colleton County from representation in the Commons House, except for Nairne. He was the only Colleton County member known to have qualified in January 1706. In fact, the Exclusion Act worked so well and so few members qualified that the Assembly had to disperse without ever formally convening.[18] Although this still-born Assembly left no official records and enacted no legislation it shed considerable light upon Carolina politics and Nairne's career.

Johnson had confounded the Dissenters and briefly dominated Carolina politics. However, his hope of purging the Commons House of all opposition was illusory. For the governor numbered among his enemies a group of "moderate" Anglicans who allied with the Dissenters and kept up opposition when their compatriots could not. Nairne was the leader and chief spokesman for this group and was one of Johnson's most powerful enemies. Lacking a distinctive title with regard to religion, Nairne and his party might best be considered Whigs—that is, Carolina counterparts of the Whig party in England.[19] In his *Journalls*, private correspondence, and *A Letter from South-Carolina*, Nairne defined the political creed of this party. He described the Carolina government in idyllic terms as one in which "the civil rights of Englishmen, together with a just, impartial, and intire liberty of Conscience, are as firmly secured to the inhabitants of this province, as acts of the general assembly can make them." The Commons House partook of "all the Powers, Priviledges, and Immunities, which the House of Commons Have in Great Britain."[20] Nairne also registered Whig values in his *Journalls* when he observed that in their government, the Chickasaws were "of the whiggish opinion that the Duties of kings and people are reciprocall that, if he failes in his they've sufficient cause to neglect their's."[21] Despite this exotic application of English political terminology, Nairne's comment upon the Chickasaws had considerable substance. In one respect it was an acute observation on the consensual character of Indian society. In another, it was a paraphrase of the rationale of the Glorious Revolution of 1689.

Governor Johnson hated and feared such political tenets, calling them among other things "antimonarchical," but he could not strike his nominal coreligionists as a group. Instead he attacked them individually, and Nairne was a prime target. Johnson issued writs for a new election immediately after the collapse of the January 1706 Assembly. Not only did the Exclusion Act do its duty, but also Johnson was reported to have interfered directly in local elections to defeat particular opponents.[22] Nairne was not reelected nor were any Colleton County members of the two previous Assemblies. The combined effect of interference and exclusion succeeded. The Assembly which met in March 1706 was Johnson's creature.

Despite the stranglehold Johnson seemed to have upon the Commons House, his grip was broken in June 1706. Carolina Dissenters, barred from office at home, shifted their attentions to England where they mounted a successful lobbying campaign against the Exclusion and Establishment Acts. Aided by the Whig journalist Daniel Defoe, they persuaded Queen Anne and the British House of Lords to disallow the two acts as "repugnant to the laws of England."[23] Johnson learned of the decision and repealed the laws in November 1706. With his compliant Assembly, he passed a new Establishment Act that carefully avoided the objectionable features of the first act and abandoned any attempt to pass a new exclusion act.

Nairne returned to the Commons House in March 1707 and quickly took a leading role. Freed from the burden of the Exclusion Act, several Dissenters took their seats and began to exercise their political strength. One of the Assembly's first actions was to compose an address of thanks to Queen Anne and the House of Lords for striking down the two offensive acts. Nairne was a member of the committee that drafted the address. In fact he claimed to have written it himself, thereby earning "the hatred of the Governor."[24] The address was largely symbolic but two other Commons House actions had direct, purposeful intent. In April 1707 Nairne helped draft "A Bill to keep inviolate and preserve the freedom of elections & ca." The bill aimed to prevent the kinds of local interference that had taken place in the March 1706 and March 1707 elections. The day after it was presented to the Commons House, Nairne introduced another bill aimed at Johnson. He proposed legislation to reform Carolina's Indian trade policies. Such reform would reduce the governor's control over the trade by depriving him of the authority to issue trading licenses. It would also deprive him of income that he customarily acquired in the form of presents from Indian tribes. Neither of these bills became law. Angered by the address and the bills, Johnson dissolved the Assembly and issued writs for a new election.[25] Despite its brevity, the April 1707 Assembly marked unmistakably the return of a strong opposition party to the Commons House.

Nairne was reelected and immediately reintroduced the reform bills of the previous Assembly. The new Assembly convened on June 5, 1707, and on June 18 a new version of the elections bill passed its first reading. On June 25 a new version of the Indian trade bill was introduced. Johnson rejected the trade bill on July 4, but that same day Nairne submitted a new version he himself had drafted. His bill was similar to the earlier trade bills but contained a provision that appropriated a £400 gratuity to Johnson and an annual stipend to the governor of £100 in lieu of gifts he had customarily received from Indians. If this amendment was a bribe, it worked. Johnson signed Nairne's Indian trade bill into law on July 19, 1707.[26]

The Indian trade act of 1707 was a new departure for the province and the beginning of a new career for Nairne. The act created a board of commissioners to regulate trade practices and to issue licenses to traders. It also established the post of Indian Agent. For a salary of £250 per year the agent was required to travel ten months of the year among the Indians dispensing justice and supervising traders among the Indian villages. His main task was to prevent traders from abusing and cheating Indians. Nairne was chosen to fill this post and quickly took up his duties.[27]

An intelligent Indian policy was essential to South Carolina. The white European minority depended for its survival upon good relations with the surrounding Indian tribes. In addition, they depended upon the Indians to sustain the province's only significant economic activity, trade with the Indians for deerskins and slaves in exchange for European goods. This trade was lucrative, especially when compared with the province's other activities, the naval stores industry, raising provisions, and the infant rice culture.[28]

Indian policy was naturally a partisan political issue. Control over the Indian trade was the only real political plum in Carolina and, consequently, was fought over with great rancor. In his first, brief term as Indian Agent Nairne could not escape this political dimension—if in fact he ever sought to do so. The politics of the Indian trade brought him near to disaster in 1708. In 1715 it killed him and nearly destroyed the province.

Nairne's first term lasted only eighteen months; and, in truth, he performed the duties of the post for less than a year. His last six months were spent locked up in the Charles Town jail charged with treason. The only accomplishment of his term was his extraordinary expedition to the Chickasaws, Talapoosas, and other Southeastern tribes.

In October 1707 Nairne arrested the trader James Child for abuses against the Indians. He charged that in 1706 Child had assembled a Cherokee raiding party and led them on a slave-catching raid against another tribe friendly to the English. Child had captured one hundred sixty Indians and sold them into slavery. In addition, several Indians had been killed during the raid. Child had powerful friends and was employed by Thomas Broughton, Governor Johnson's son-in-law. Child claimed that he had a commission from Johnson to conduct the raid, making it a public venture like Nairne's 1702 Florida raid. In Nairne's eyes, this made Johnson an accomplice in an unlawful and unwise war against friendly Indians. He confronted Johnson on another trade issue when he seized one thousand deerskins for the public, which skins Johnson claimed were his personal property.[29]

Nairne's zealous management brought quick retribution. Johnson transformed the Commons House investigation of Child into an inquiry into Nairne's conduct as Indian Agent. In November 1707 Johnson sent to the Assembly depositions by two traders alleging that Nairne had "degraded" him in talks with Indians, calling him "an old fool."[30] When the Commons House was prorogued on November 28, 1707, Nairne, not Child, was in a difficult position. It was under these conditions that he and his colleague Thomas Welch, an Indian trader among the Chickasaws, undertook their notable journey to the west.

Thomas Nairne's Indian Agency occurred at a critical time, not only for Carolina, but also for all of the European settlements in North America. His 1708 expedition must be understood in a larger context than Carolina politics or trade policies. It originated in the struggle for hegemony in North America between France, Spain, and England. The War of the Spanish Succession began in 1702 and concluded in 1713 with the Treaty of Utrecht. In Europe, for the most part, professional armies fought one another in formal battles with elaborate strategies and maneuvers, and clear winners. Many of the battles were in truth sieges, employing complex fortifications and techniques. The American phase of the war, called Queen Anne's War, was different. Much of the actual fighting was done by Indian armies commanded by a few Europeans. Battles consisted of raids and counterraids upon European settlements or upon those of allied Indians. The Carolinians' attack upon St. Augustine in 1702 and Governor James Moore's campaign in 1704 against the Apalachee Indians in Florida were examples of this type of warfare.[31] The joint French and Spanish seaborne assault upon Charles Town in August 1706 was an exception to this rule of warfare. Planned and executed solely by Europeans it partook of the Continental manner.[32] Its failure demonstrated the tactical and logistical problems of such large-scale enterprises. For the remainder of the war in the Southeast, battles were fought on a smaller scale by Indian proxies.

In August and September 1707 Carolinians retaliated for the Charles Town invasion by conducting raids against the Spanish and Spanish-allied Indians on the Apalachee and Chattahoochee Rivers. The raiders were Alabama and Talapoosa Indians led by a few whites. This army burned the town of Pensacola but, as in 1702 against St. Augustine, failed to capture the presidio.[33]

In October 1707 rumors reached Charles Town that the French at Fort Louis de la Louisiane (Old Mobile) were planning to assemble an Indian army to attack Carolina overland. This news prompted Nairne and Thomas Welch to propose a plan to strike against Mobile. Nairne designed to isolate the French at Mobile by seducing their Indian allies in the Southeast, notably the powerful and numerous Choctaws. If the French Indians could not be won over to the English they were to be exterminated by an Indian army collected and led by Nairne. The Commons House approved the plan and on November 7, 1707, commissioned Nairne and Welch to undertake a diplomatic mission to the French Indians and, if necessary, to conduct a war of extermination.[34] This was the origin and purpose of Nairne's western expedition. His *Journalls*, a record of that expedition, was filled with ethnographical data and acute observations upon Indian and white societies. However, these were of decidedly secondary importance to Nairne and his contemporaries. The *Journalls* was primarily the record of a secret diplomatic mission that, if it had succeeded, would have drenched the Southeast in blood.

The two men set out from Charles Town at the beginning of 1708. By January 20 they had reached "Ogfaskee," the chief town of the Talapoosas, on the west bank of the Tallapoosa River. In April they were among the Chickasaws, in present-day northeastern Mississippi. At that point Welch traveled west to the bank of the Mississippi River where he met the Natchez, Tensas, and Yazoo Indians. Nairne traveled south to negotiate with the Choctaws. According to a French report of his visit, Nairne met the Choctaws at their chief town, gave them presents, and asked them "to aid them to destroy all the small nations that were nearest to our fort [at Mobile]—the Tomeh, Mobile, Tawasa, Chato, Pascagoula, and Pensacola who are not more than ten leagues away from us."[35]

Nairne and Welch returned to Charles Town in May or June of 1708 and reported success. Perhaps that was the reason their expedition had not turned into a military campaign. But, whether or not they succeeded, their plan was never implemented. Rumors of another joint French-Spanish assault upon Charles Town forced the Carolinians to postpone the offensive and concentrate upon defending the metropolis. The attack never came but the postponement became permanent when the politics of faction ensnared Nairne.

Thomas Nairne was arrested on June 24, 1708, charged with "High Treason in Endeavouring to disinherit and Dethrone our Rightfull and Lawfull Sovereigne Lady Queen Ann, and to place in her Person the pretended Prince of Wales."[36] His arrest, long imprisonment without trial, escape from Carolina, and subsequent vindication in England are high political drama. Unfortunately, the only extant records of the event were written by Nairne or his sympathizers and present very one-sided accounts.[37] If there was any merit to Johnson's charge, no substantial evidence has been found. Nairne presented his case in letters to the Earl of Sunderland and in petitions to Queen Anne and William, Lord Craven, the Proprietary Palatine of Carolina. According to Nairne, Johnson had fabricated the treason charge to destroy a powerful political opponent and to preserve his control over the Indian trade. He characterized Johnson's supposed witnesses against him as "lewd fellows . . . Influenced to serve a Turn, one being a Lunatick and the other a meer Villain . . . put in prison for Buggery."[38] The treason charge had been built up over time and was based upon depositions by witnesses that they had overheard Nairne utter Jacobite sentiments on two separate occasions half a year apart. In November 1707, in the midst of the James Child investigation, Johnson presented depositions to the Commons House by two unnamed traders concerning Nairne's contemptuous statements regarding the governor. These depositions had obliged Nairne to begin his western expedition under a cloud of suspicion.

Upon his return to Charles Town in the spring of 1708 the old charges had been embellished by the two deponents into high treason against Queen Anne. In a petition to the Queen, Nairne said the "Lunatick" and "meer Villain . . . Swore that your petitioner had said that the pretended Prince of Wales was Son to the Late King and Rt. Heir to the Crown which they Deposed to have been spoken in the Woods in Novbr. 1707, and did not make their Depositions untill June ye 17th, 1708." This remark, reported seven months after it had allegedly occurred, was the occasion for his arrest.[39] Moreover, a second incident, contemptuously called by Nairne his "new Treason," occurred while he was in the Charles Town jail. "An illiterate fellow one Hakes" reported to Johnson that in a conversation between Nairne and the Rev. Edward Marston, Nairne had "averred the Queen had no tittle to the Crown but the Prince of Wales had."[40] Marston, a strong hater of Johnson in his own right, testified before the governor and his Council that Hakes' statement was false.[41]

Despite all of the alleged evidence against Nairne, he was never brought to trial. Indeed he speculated that Johnson never intended to try him but to hold him in prison until he succumbed to disease or was financially ruined. Johnson claimed that he had postponed trying Nairne in order to receive instructions from the Lords Proprietors as to how the case was to be handled, but he did not request any instructions until April 1709.[42] By then Nairne had been released from jail, left the province, and was in London pleading his case in person before the Lords Proprietors.

During his imprisonment Nairne composed his notable memorial of July 10, 1708 to the Earl of Sunderland, drew his map of the Southeast, and was reelected to the Commons House of Assembly. His reelection proved to be his ticket out of jail. He was released upon orders of the Commons House to participate in an investigation to learn whether he could sit in the Commons House while under indictment for treason. The investigating committee was weighed heavily against Nairne. Only two of its seven members were from Colleton County. Despite that, the committee had difficulty reaching a decision and asked Governor Johnson for guidance. He replied that the Commons House was the sole judge of the case but that he expected Nairne to be expelled. Nairne testified in his defense on December 2, 1708, and later that day the committee recommended his expulsion. The Assembly immediately voted not to admit Nairne to his seat and called upon Johnson to issue a writ of election to replace him. It also voted not to enter into its journal the reason for Nairne's expulsion and refused to permit Nairne's supporters to record their dissents.[43]

The next day Nairne ran afoul of the Commons House over the conduct of his Indian Agency. He petitioned to be paid part of his salary but another committee studying his claims learned of the existence of his map of the Southeast. This new committee contained four members, a majority, who had only the day before recommended Nairne's expulsion. It ordered Nairne to produce his map, but he refused, saying that he had sent it to Lord Sunderland. Having been removed from his Commons House seat and then forced to haggle over his salary, Nairne was not inclined to cooperate with the Assembly. He saucily replied that "he would consider before he laid before this House the Mapp he had drawn of the Indian Country."[44] For this answer he was arrested by the Commons House for contempt and removed from his post as Indian Agent. Nairne posted bond to obtain his release and some time between December 1708 and April 1709 "absconded" to England to plead his case before the Lords Proprietors.[45]

In London Nairne exculpated himself from the treason charge and was appointed by the Lords Proprietors to be a vice admiralty judge of Carolina. It is likely that during his stay he also made arrangements with Edward Crisp or with the Proprietors to publish his map of the Southeast and his "New Chart" as part of Crisp's "Compleat Description of Carolina." He also probably wrote and arranged for the publication of A Letter from South-Carolina. When Nairne returned to Carolina is not known. He reappeared in the public records in November 1711 when he was elected to the Commons House.[46]

The most notable event that occurred during Nairne's absence was the removal from office of Nathaniel Johnson. Governor Johnson had made himself notorious to the Lords Proprietors for his exclusion policy and other acts of high-handedness. In December 1708 the Proprietors commissioned Edward Tynte to replace Johnson. Tynte arrived in Charles Town in November 1709 but died within six months.[47] Lieutenant Governor Robert Gibbes succeeded Tynte and held office until April 1712. In that month he was replaced by Charles Craven, a nephew of the Proprietor Lord William Craven. Charles Craven proved to be the best governor of the Proprietary era.[48]

Nairne returned to the Commons House in November 1711 to fill a vacant Colleton County seat. His return to that uncomfortable arena was likely prompted by a sense of duty. A week earlier Carolinians had learned of the outbreak of the Tuscarora War in North Carolina. Partisan politics abated during the war crisis and the accession of Governor Craven assured Nairne a congenial climate during his final term in the Commons House. For nearly a year he was a busy legislator instead of a party leader. He sponsored bills on a variety of subjects, including road building, control of infectious diseases, the appointment of a colonial agent "to solicit the affairs of this Province in Great Britain," and even a bill to construct a governor's mansion. He also helped to draft the reception statute of 1712.[49] This law incorporated a wide range of English statutes into Carolina's legal system. It placed the province upon a firm statutory basis as an English colony and consequently weakened the Proprietors' autonomous authority.

While in the Commons House, Nairne did not neglect Indian affairs. In addition to his work during the Tuscarora War he drafted an act to establish a reservation on Palawana Island for the Cusabo Indians. He was appointed a special commissioner to his neighbors the Yemassee and in December 1712 resumed his duties as the province's Indian Agent.[50] Barred from membership in the Commons House during his agency, Nairne resigned from the Assembly in December 1712 and never returned to that body.

Although Nairne never repeated his 1708 western excursion he took an active interest in western expansion schemes. One of these schemes was the design of the Welshman Pryce Hughes to replace the French settlements in Louisiana with an English colony called "Annarea." Hughes had likely made Nairne's acquaintance in England and the latter had assisted Hughes and other Welsh immigrants to obtain land in Carolina. Hughes arrived in Carolina in 1712 and immediately set out on travels throughout the Southeast. He was "An English Gent. who had a particular fancy of rambling among the Indians" and soon made himself, briefly, the most active spokesman in Carolina for British expansionism.[51] Back in Charles Town after an extended "ramble," Hughes consulted Nairne and sought his aid to establish "Annarea."

Hughes campaigned against the Choctaws in April 1714, at the head of an army of Chickasaws, Alabamas, and Talapoosas. Without bloodshed, he and his army momentarily lured the Choctaws from the French allegiance through a combination of threats and presents. For a moment it seemed as though Nairne's plan, as set out in his memorial, was on the verge of success. But on his third expedition Hughes' luck ran out. He was captured by the French, interrogated for three days at Fort St. Louis by Jean Baptiste Le Moyne, Sieur de Bienville, and released. Returning home alone, he briefly visited the Spanish at Pensacola and headed for Charles Town. En route he was captured and killed in April 1715 by a party of Tohome Indians.[52] Hughes' death was nearly simultaneous with Nairne's. The great uprising known as the Yemassee War had begun.

Despite his years of dedication to Indian trade reform, Nairne's efforts came to nought. Abuses of Indians by deerskin and slave traders were endemic in these exploitive activities and no amount of supervision or post facto reparations could meliorate them. Although he labored hard to redress Indians' grievance and to reform the system, Nairne could not halt the looming disaster and, ironically, he was one of its first victims. On April 14, 1715, William Bray, Samuel Warner, and Thomas Nairne rendezvoused at the Yemassee town of Pocataligo. Bray and Warner had brought warning to Charles Town of a planned Indian uprising and had been despatched to Pocataligo to head it off. Nairne learned of the plan while at his plantation on St. Helena Island and hastened to Pocataligo on his own. The three men hoped to redress some of the Yemassees' grievances but their efforts were too little, too late. They awakened on Good Friday, April 15, 1715, to the sounds of war cries. The Yemassee killed Bray and Warner outright and captured Nairne. They then tortured him by fire, sticking lightwood splinters into his body and igniting them. According to contemporary reports, Nairne lived for three days before he finally succumbed. These events were the first blows of the Yemassee War which lasted for two years and threatened the survival of the English settlements in Carolina.[53]

Thomas Nairne's *Journalls to the Chicasaws and Talapoosies* is part of the manuscript collections of the British Library. Accessioned as Additional Manuscript 42559, it is titled "Accounts of North American Indians" in the British Library's printed catalog of manuscripts.[54] The *Journalls* is an eighteenth-century copy of four letters from Nairne to the Board of Commissioners of the Indian Trade at Charles Town. Dated January 20, April 12, 13, and 15, 1708, the letters were written from the Talapoosa town of "Ogfaskee" and the Chickasaw town of "Hollachatroe." At a later date the letters were copied, bound into a journal of forty-seven numbered folios, and assigned the title "Capt. Thomas Nairne's Journalls to the Chicasaws and Talapoosies." The copyist gave titles to three of the letters and added marginal catch-phrases to the manuscript volume. These additions accorded with established usages both for book publication and the preservation of official British documents. They transformed Nairne's four letters into an epistolary journal. Nairne's original letters were lost and the *Journalls* is the only surviving text.

Nairne's *Journalls* recounted his and Thomas Welch's secret diplomatic mission during war time more than seven hundred miles into Indian territory. It also recorded a wealth of ethnographical information on the customs, ceremonies, and social organizations of the Chickasaws, Talapoosas, and Ochese Indian tribes. Nairne's description of the Chickasaw rank of *fane mingo* is an ethnographical first that explains much about intertribal relations and the mechanics of Indian-white diplomacy. Another example of Nairne's careful recording and thoughtful analysis of Indian customs is his account of the "coronation" of Cossitee, the "Ogfaskee Captain." As recorded by Nairne, the ceremony was an adaptation of a traditional Creek ceremony to the uses of Anglo-Indian diplomacy, a classic example of the process of acculturation.[55]

As a literary production, Nairne's *Journalls* reveals much about the author's character and background. *A Letter from South-*

Carolina demonstrated Nairne's political acumen and his strongly Whiggish ideas. The *Journalls* reinforces these perceptions. It also reveals his educational attainments, his ironic wit, and his lyrical turn of phrase. Seven hundred miles from Charles Town, in the midst of war-plotting, Nairne mused upon the natural history and geography of the Chickasaw homelands in terms that evoked the landscape of a Biblical "peaceable kingdom."

> It's now that season of the year, when nature adorns the Earth in a livery of verdant green, and there is some pleasure in an evening to ride up and down the savannas. When among a Tuft of Oak's or on a riseing knowll, in the midst of a Large grassy plain, I revolve a thousand things about the primitive life of men and think how finely on such a small Hill the tents might stand and from thence men have the agreeable sight of the Flocks feeding around them. Thus lived and rambled the great Patriarch in the plains of the East, thus stood the tents under and about the Oakes of Mamre.[56]

Unfortunately the *Journalls* suffers from numerous textual problems. Its provenance is largely unknown. The unknown copyist, writing hastily and only partly comprehending what he read, misspelled, misread, and omitted words and phrases. The surviving text is therefore badly corrupted. Only a few circumstantial clues can be found to suggest the identity of the copyist. It is certain that the handwriting in the *Journalls* is not that of Nairne.

Proceeding in a detective-like fashion it is possible to make some circumstantial assumptions about the identity of the copyist. Only a few men in Carolina had motive and opportunity to make a copy and then carry it to England. Among these few, Richard Beresford of Goose Creek in Berkeley County fits the clues best. In 1708 Beresford was a member of the Board of Commissioners of the Indian Trade, one of the men to whom Nairne's letters were directed. In the latter phases of the Yemassee War, Beresford and Joseph Boone, a long-time colonial agent for Carolina, were sent to Great Britain to solicit aid for rebuilding the colony and repairing the ravages of the Yemassees.[57] Beresford met the Lords Proprietors and crown officials during his stay in London and presented several memorials to the Board of Trade. These memorials not only set forth Carolina's pitiable condition but also argued, in language similar to Nairne's memorial of July 1708 to Sunderland, for a concerted campaign to drive the French and Spanish from the Southeast.[58]

Along with this circumstantial evidence, perhaps the most compelling link between Nairne, Beresford and the *Journalls*, is Beresford's reputation as a cartographer and informant for the cartographer Herman Moll. Among the map collections of the British Public Record Office is an untitled manuscript map, assigned the descriptive title of "Indian Tribes of the Southeast." This map is traditionally called the "Richard Beresford Map," and it is believed that Beresford either drew the map or provided information for its composition. This Beresford map is an earlier, less complete version of the famous John Barnwell map of the Southeast, *circa* 1722. There is some evidence, though not conclusive, that several annotations on the Beresford map are in the handwriting of the copyist of Nairne's *Journalls*.[59] Another bit of cartographical evidence is found on Herman Moll's "A New Map of the North Parts of America Claimed by France." In the legend of this map, Moll acknowledged the "Original Draughts of . . . the Ingenious Mr. Beresford, now residing in Carolina, Capt. Nearn, and others."[60]

Despite these circumstantial clues, there is no conclusive evidence that Beresford copied Nairne's *Journalls*. Verifiable samples of Beresford's handwriting cannot be found in the South Carolina Department of Archives and History or in the British Public Record Office. Until such a comparison of handwritings is made or a better circumstantial candidate is identified, the copyist's identity must remain unknown.

With one exception Nairne's *Journalls* has gone unnoticed and unused by historians, anthropologists, and literary historians since it was first compiled. The exception was David Baillie Warden, a Scot who emigrated to the United States, had a brief diplomatic career, and devoted his life to American historical bibliography and statistics. In 1819 Warden published *A Statistical, Political, and Historical Account of the United States of North America; From the Period of their First Colonization to the Present Day*. In his section on the Alabama Territory Warden cited among "Books and

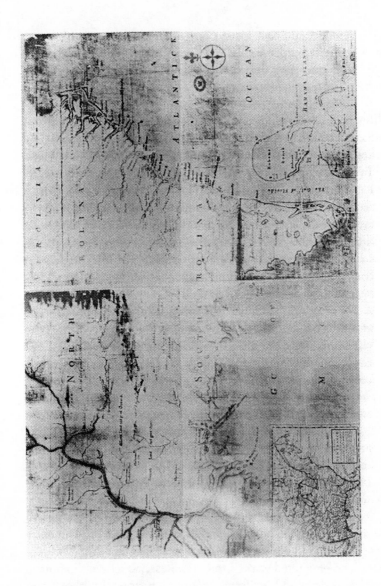

Map 3

Richard Beresford, Map of North and South Carolina and Florida, *circa* 1715, C.O. 700, North American Colonies, 3. Reproduced from A.B. Hulbert, *Crown Collection of Photographs of American Maps* (Cleveland, Ohio: Arthur H. Clark, 1904–1916), Series III, plates 13–16, with permission of the Keeper of Public Records, Great Britain Public Record Office.

Documents relating to this Territory" a work he called a "Survey By Captain Mairn [*sic*] of Carolina," dated 1708.[61] How Warden might have learned of the *Journalls* is not known; whether he saw it in Edinburgh, where the *History* was published, or in Paris, his home, or in the United States, or Great Britain, is also a mystery. Despite this mystery, Warden's mention of it adds an important link in the provenance of the *Journalls*.

Because of the poor textual quality of the *Journalls* no extraordinary efforts have been made to reproduce the text exactly as written. Instead, the expanded style of historical editing, described in the *Harvard Guide to American History*, has been employed to render intelligible a poor text.[62] The copyist's spelling has been retained throughout within the guidelines of the expanded style. However, in some cases, notably proper nouns, alternative readings have been supplied in brackets within the text. Two major emendations have been made in the *Journalls*. The random order of the letters as copied in the *Journalls* has been altered to a chronological one and the copyist's catch-phrases have been omitted.

Notes

1. Verner W. Crane's *The Southern Frontier, 1670–1732* (Durham, N.C.: Duke University Press, 1928) is the best account of Nairne's life and death. M. Eugene Sirmans, *Colonial South Carolina, A Political History, 1663–1763* (Chapel Hill; University of North Carolina Press, 1966) and Alexander Moore, "Carolina Whigs: Colleton County Members of the South Carolina Commons House of Assembly, 1692–1720" (Master's thesis, University of South Carolina, 1981) recount his political career. *Dictionary of American Biography*, 1955 ed., s.v. "Thomas Nairne" by Verner W. Crane and Walter B. Edgar and N. Louise Bailey, eds., *Biographical Directory of the South Carolina House of Representatives*, 4 vols. (Columbia: University of South Carolina Press, 1974–1984), 2:491–492, are also useful.

2. *A Letter from South-Carolina; Giving an Account of the Soil, Air, Product, Trade, Government, Laws, Religion, People, Military Strength, &c. of that Province. Together with the Manner and Necessary Charges of Settling a Plantation there, and the Annual Profit it will produce. Written by a Swiss Gentleman, to his Friend at Bern* (London: A. Baldwin, 1710; 2nd ed. R. Smith, 1718 and J. Clarke, 1732). *A Letter* was also published in *North-Carolina University Magazine* 4 (September 1855):289–305. The John Carter Brown Library, Providence, R.I., owns an un-

dated, unsigned, autograph draft by Nairne of portions of A Letter. The ms. has 18 numbered quarto pages and is entitled "A Description of Carolina." A collation with the 1710 edition of A Letter reveals that the ms. lacks material that appears on printed pp. 3–6, 58–63 and a few short, scattered passages. See Joseph Sabin and others, A Dictionary of Books Relating to America from Its Discovery to the Present Time, 29 vols. (New York: Joseph Sabin and Others, 1868–1936), 22: nos. 87859–61 for Nairne's authorship of A Letter.

3. Thomas Nairne to [Charles Spencer, Earl of Sunderland], July 10, 1708, in Great Britain Public Record Office, London, Colonial Office 5:382, no. 11 (British Manuscripts Project, reel D444, microfilm in South Carolina Department of Archives and History, Columbia, S.C.). The memorial has been published in Cecil Headlam, ed., Calendar of State Papers, Colonial Series, America and West Indies, Volume 24, June 1708–1709 (London: HMSO, 1922), pp. 421–424. A facsimile edition of an 1890s transcription is in Records in the British Public Record Office Relating to South Carolina, Volume 5, 1701–1710 (Columbia: State Historical Commission, 1947), pp. 193–202. Because of its signal importance to Nairne's career and his Journalls the memorial is republished herein. The diplomatic character of Nairne's Journalls is discussed in Alexander Moore, "Thomas Nairne's 1708 Western Expedition: An Episode in the Anglo-French Competition for Empire," in Proceedings of the Tenth Annual Meeting of the French Colonial Historical Society, ed. Philip M. Boucher (Washington: University Press of America, 1985), pp. 47–58.

4. Edward Crisp, "A Compleat Description of the Province of Carolina in 3 Parts," in William P. Cumming, The Southeast in Early Maps (Chapel Hill: University of North Carolina Press, 1962), plates 44, 45, and pp. 40–41, 179–180. Nairne's inset of the Southeast is reproduced as a frontispiece in this edition of the Journalls. The "New Chart" is primarily a coasting map with harbor and channel soundings. See John Carter Brown Annual Reports, 1901–1966, 5 vols. (Providence, R.I.: John Carter Brown Library, 1972), 5:10–17, and 6:36–39, for information on the Crisp map and Nairne insets.

5. Herman Moll, "A New Map of the North Parts of America Claimed by France under the Names of Louisiana, Mississippi, Canada and New France with adjoining Territories of England and Spain, 1720," is reproduced as map two herein. For its place in American cartography and of Nairne's influence upon Moll's work see Cumming, Southeast in Early Maps, pp. 43–44, 81, and Cumming and others, The Exploration of North America, 1630–1776 (New York: Putnam, 1974), pp. 94–95. Moll's 1715 map is described in Cumming, Southeast in Early Maps, pp. 181–183.

6. One Thomas Nairne, perhaps a forbear, represented Forres in the Scottish Parliament in 1649. For Nairne's Scottish nationality see Alexander Moore, "'A Narrative of an Assembly . . . January the 2d, 1705/6': New Light on Early South Carolina Politics," South Carolina Historical Magazine 85 (July 1984): 181–186, and George F. Black, The Surnames of Scotland (New York: New York Public Library, 1946), p. 623.

7. Will of Richard Quintyne, January 26, 1694/5, in Wills, Inventories, and Miscellaneous Documents (WPA Transcripts), Vol. 60, 1692–1695, pp. 263–268 (at Sc-Ar) and Alexander S. Salley, ed., "Abstracts from the Records of the Court of Ordinary of the Province of South Carolina, 1692–1700," *SCHM* 10 (April 1909): 83–84.

8. Will of Elizabeth Nairne, March 3, 1720/21 (recorded May 23, 1722), Charleston County Will Book, 1721–1722 (WPA Transcript), p. 4; Inventory of the Estate of Elizabeth Nairne, October 19, 1722 (recorded November 19, 1722) in Wills, Inventories, and Miscellaneous Records, 1722–1724 (WPA Transcripts), Vol. 66, pp. 22–23. See "The Bull Family of South Carolina," *SCHM* 1 (January 1900):79, for her genealogy and Anne King Gregorie, ed., *Records of the Court of Chancery of South Carolina, 1671–1799* (Washington: American Historical Association, 1950; reprint ed., Millwood, N.Y.: Kraus Reprint Co., 1975), pp. 202–203 and 237–239, for 1717 litigation between Elizabeth Nairne and her sons-in-law William Bull and Thomas Murray concerning the estate of her son Henry Quintyne.

9. Robert Ellis to James Petiver, April 25, 1704, British Library, London, Additional Ms. 4064, Sloane Manuscripts (microfilm in South Carolina Historical Society, Charleston, S.C.). See Records of the Secretary of the Province, Land Grants, Colonial Series of Royal Grants, (ms. vols. at Sc-Ar), Vol. 38:434–435; 39:4, 17, 156, 438–439, 442–443, 494–496, for Nairne's land acquisitions.

10. Thomas Nairne, Jr., is buried beside his mother in St. Andrews Church-yard, Charleston County, S.C. "Inscriptions from St. Andrews Church Yard," *SCHM* 13 (April 1912):117.

11. Nairne, *A Letter from South-Carolina*, pp. 4, 43.

12. See map two, Cumming, *Southeast in Early Maps*, p. 80, and Nairne to Edward Marston, August 20, 1705, in United Society for the Propagation of the Gospel in Foreign Parts, London, Society for the Propagation of the Gospel Mss., Letters, Series A, vol. 2, no. 156 (published microfilm in Thomas Cooper Library, University of South Carolina, Columbia).

13. *The Statutes at Large of South Carolina*, ed. by Thomas Cooper and David J. McCord, 10 vols. (Columbia, S.C.: A.S. Johnston, 1837–1873), 2: no. 269.

14. At a ratio of £6.1 Carolina money to one pound sterling, Elizabeth Nairne's estate was worth £601.49 sterling, of which £441 was in slaves. Her total wealth ranked extremely low among Carolina planters but her 27 slaves placed her among the upper one-eighth of slave owners in the province. According to the most readily available estimates slaves constituted about 45% of a Carolina planter's wealth in the 1720s. Elizabeth Nairne's proportion was nearer to 72%. In other words, she had little wealth other than her slaves. See William G. Bentley, "Wealth Distribution in Colonial South Carolina" (Ph.D. dissertation, Georgia State University, 1977), table 7, p. 35, and table 55, p. 82.

15. Commons House Journals of the South Carolina General Assembly, 1692–1721, 17 ms. vols. at Sc-Ar (hereinafter Commons House Journals), Vol. 11:343, 346–347, 353, for Nairne's activities during the Tuscarora War.

16. Moore, "Narrative of an Assembly," p. 184.

17. *Statutes*, 2: nos. 222 and 225, respectively the Exclusion and Establishment Acts.

18. Moore, "Narrative of an Assembly," pp. 181–186.

19. John Robert Moore, "Defoe's 'Queries upon the Foregoing Act': A Defense of Civil Liberty in South Carolina," in *Essays in History and Literature Presented by Fellows of the Newberry Library to Stanley Pargellis*, ed. Heinz Bluhm (Chicago: Newberry Library, 1965), pp. 133–155, and Moore, "Carolina Whigs," *passim*, place South Carolina politics in a British party context.

20. Nairne, *A Letter from South-Carolina*, pp. 18, 22.

21. Thomas Nairne, *Journalls to the Chicasaws and Talapoosies*, p. 39 herein. See also Thomas Nairne to Henry Compton, Bishop of London, n.d., enclosed in Robert Stevens to the Secretary of the S.P.G., February 3, 1708, SPG Mss., Letters, Series A, vol. 4, no. 19.

22. Commons House Journals, 5:16–17; Moore, "Carolina Whigs," p. 130.

23. Moore, "Defoe's 'Queries,'" pp. 151–153; *Journals of the House of Lords, Beginning Anno Quarto Anne Regnae, 1705* (London: n.d.), 18:138–144; Great Britain Historical Manuscripts Commission *Report No. 14*, Vol. 6, new series, *The Manuscripts of the House of Lords, 1704–1706* (London: HMSO, 1912), pp. 409–410; Queen Anne's Orders in Council, June 10, 1706, C.O.5:1291, pp. 394–395.

24. Commons House Journals, 7:69–73; Thomas Nairne to [Earl of Sunderland], July 28, 1708, C.O.5:306, pp. 10–11, published in *Calendar of State Papers, Colonial Series, America and West Indies*, Vol. 24, no. 662.

25. Commons House Journals, 7:48, 61, 63, 69–73.

26. Commons House Journals, 8:233, 277, 302–304, 342–343; *Statutes*, 2: no. 269.

27. *Ibid.*

28. Converse D. Clowse, *Economic Beginnings in Colonial South Carolina, 1670–1730* (Columbia, S.C.: University of South Carolina Press, 1971), *passim*; Philip M. Brown, "Early Indian Trade in the Development of South Carolina: Politics, Economics, and Social Mobility during the Proprietary Era," SCHM 76 (July 1977):118–128; Richard L. Haan, "The 'Trade Do's Not Flourish as Formerly': The Ecological Origins of the Yamassee War of 1715," *Ethnohistory* 28 (Fall 1982):341–358; Crane, *Southern Frontier*, Chapter V, "The Charles Town Indian Trade."

29. Nairne to [Sunderland], July 28, 1708, C.O.5:306, pp.10–11; Petition of Thomas Nairne to William, Lord Craven, [ca. October 1708], in Henry E. Huntington Library and Art Gallery, San Marino, Ca., Documents Relating to the Treason Trial of Thomas Nairne (hereinafter Nairne Mss.).

30. Commons House Journals, 9:63–64.

31. Mark Boyd and others, *Here They Once Stood: The Tragic End of the Apalachee Missions* (Gainesville, Fla.: University of Florida Press, 1951), *passim*; Boyd, "Further Considerations of the Apalachee Missions," *The Americas* 9 (April 1953):459–479; Nairne to Marston, August 20, 1705, in SPG Mss., Letters, Series

A, vol. 2, no. 156; Charles W. Arnade, *The Siege of St. Augustine in 1702* (Gainesville, Fla.: University of Florida Press, 1959), *passim*.

32. "An Account of the Invasion of South Carolina by the French & Spaniards in the Month of August 1706," C.O.5:382, pp. 20-22; *Boston News-Letter*, October 14, 1706; Kenneth R. Jones, ed., "'A Full and Particular Account' of the Assault on Charleston in 1706," *SCHM* 83 (January 1982):1-11.

33. Stanley Faye, "The Contest for Pensacola, 1700-1706," *Florida Historical Quarterly* 25 (1945-46):167-195, 302-328; Jay Higginbotham, *Old Mobile, Fort Louis de la Louisiane, 1702-1711* (Mobile, Ala.: Museum of the City of Mobile, 1977), pp. 307-313.

34. Alexander S. Salley, ed., *Journal of the Commons House of Assembly of South Carolina, October 22, 1707-February 12, 1707/8* (Columbia: State Historical Commission, 1941), pp. 10-11, 33-34, 48-50.

35. Moore, "Thomas Nairne's Western Expedition," p. 52.

36. Nathaniel Johnson to John Collins, June 24, 1708, Mittimus to arrest Thomas Nairne, Nairne Mss.

37. In addition to the Nairne Mss. there are two items in the British Library, Additional Ms. 61623, ff. 51-54 (part of the Blenheim Manuscripts). One is an undated petition by Nairne to Queen Anne, a duplicate of a petition in the Nairne Mss. The other is a letter from Nairne to the Earl of Sunderland, December 10, 1708, discussing his western design and his imprisonment. Other Nairne letters and papers are in the British Public Record Office and the Records of the Society for the Propagation of the Gospel, London, England.

38. Petition to Queen Anne, n.d., Nairne Mss.; copy in BL, Add. Ms. 61623, ff. 53-54.

39. *Ibid.*

40. Petition to Queen Anne, n.d.; Nairne to the Earl of Sunderland, October 10, 1708; and Deposition of George Smith, September 22, 1708, all in Nairne Mss. See also James D. Alsop, "Thomas Nairne and the 'Boston Gazette No. 216,' of 1707," *Southern Studies* 22 (Summer 1983):209-211. Lacking access to the Nairne Mss. Alsop misconstrued the character of the charges against Nairne.

41. Deposition of George Smith, September 22, 1708, Nairne Mss. and Edward Marston, *To the Most Noble Henry Duke of Beaufort Marquis and Earl of Worcester, Baron Herbert, Lord of Ragland, Chepstow and Gower. Palatine of the Province of South Carolina in America* (London: 1712) for Marston's animosities toward Nathaniel Johnson.

42. Nairne to Sunderland, July 28, 1708, in C.O.5:306, p. 10; Minutes of Lords Proprietors' Meeting, April 14, 1709, in C.O. 5:292, p. 15.

43. Commons House Journals, 10:88-89, 92-98, quote on p. 98.

44. *Ibid.*, pp. 98, 102-103, 108, quote on p. 106.

45. *Ibid.*, p. 158.

46. Minutes of Lords Proprietors' Meeting, February 28, 1710/11, in C.O.5:292, p. 44. Nairne attended a meeting on July 27, 1710, and his admiralty appointment was discussed on June 6, 1711. *Ibid.*, pp. 34, 46. *A Letter from South-*

Carolina bears the dateline "Charlestown. June 1, 1710" but the dateline is apocryphal.

47. Alexander S. Salley, ed., *Commissions and Instructions from the Lords Proprietors of Carolina to Public Officials of South Carolina, 1685–1715* (Columbia: State Historical Commission, 1916), pp. 224–226, for Tynte's commission. See also John Raimo, *Biographical Directory of American Colonial and Revolutionary Governors, 1607–1789* (Westport, Conn.: Meckler Books, 1980), s.v. "Edward Tynte."

48. *Ibid.*, s.v. "Robert Gibbes" and "Charles Craven."

49. Commons House Journals, 11:350, 509; Commons House Journals (John S. Green Transcript), 4:109–110, 123, 167. For Nairne's sponsorship of road building and construction of a governor's mansion see Commons House Journals, 11:350, 509. The reception act of 1712 is found in *Statutes*, 2: no. 328.

50. For Nairne's activities during the Tuscarora War see p. 19 herein and note 15. See Commons House Journals (Green Transcript), 4:115–116, 119–120, 124, 130–131, 146, for the Palawana reservation act and Nairne's Indian agencies.

51. Crane, *Southern Frontier*, pp. 99–107, contains a good account of Pryce Hughes' brief career. See also Pryce Hughes to Thomas Nairne, *ca.* 1713, in Pryce Hughes Letters from South Carolina Proposing a Welsh Colony, 1713, in South Caroliniana Library, University of South Carolina. Alexander Spotswood's comment is in *The Official Letters of Alexander Spotswood, Lieutenant Governor of the Colony of Virginia, 1710–1722*, ed. Robert A. Brock, 2 vols. (Richmond: Virginia Historical Society, 1882–1885), 2:331.

52. Crane, *Southern Frontier*, p. 107. John Barnwell's [Southeastern North America, *ca.* 1722] marks the site of Hughes' murder. See Cumming, *Southeast in Early Maps*, plate 48 and pp. 45–47, 190.

53. Crane, *Southern Frontier*, pp. 168–169; William L. McDowell, ed., *Journals of the Commissioners of the Indian Trade, September 20, 1710–August 29, 1718* (Columbia: University of South Carolina Press, 1955), p. 65.

54. British Library, *Catalogue of Additions to the Manuscripts, 1931–1935* (London: British Museum, 1967), p. 43.

55. For the term *fane mingo* see text note 20.

56. *Journalls*, p. 58.

57. Ella Lonn, *The Colonial Agents of the Southern Colonies* (Chapel Hill: University of North Carolina Press, 1945), pp. 66–70, 184–185, 187, 233; *Biographical Directory of the S.C. House of Representatives*, 2:77–78.

58. A memorial by Beresford and his fellow agent Joseph Boone of June 16, 1716, is printed in William S. Saunders, ed., *The Colonial Records of North Carolina*, 10 vols. (Raleigh, N.C.: Josephus Daniels, 1890), 2:229–234. Another memorial by Beresford, "The Designs of the French to Extend their Settlements from Canada to the Mississippi behind the British Plantations," is in C.O.5:327, no. 7. It strongly echoes Nairne's *Journalls* and memorial.

59. Beresford's map is filed in the British Public Record Office in Colonial Office 700, North American Colonies, 3, and is reproduced herein as map 3. Comments on the map, rather than place names and Indian names, are in a handwriting very similar to the copyist's hand in the *Journalls.* See Cumming, *Southeast in Early Maps,* pp. 43–44, 181.

60. See frontispiece and Cumming, *Exploration of North America,* pp. 94–95.

61. David Baillie Warden, *A Statistical, Political, and Historical Account of the United States of North America; From the Period of their First Colonization to the Present Day.* 3 vols. (Edinburgh: Archibald Constable and Co., 1819), 3:41.

62. "The Care and Editing of Manuscripts," in *Harvard Guide to American History,* ed. Frank Freidel, 2 vols. (revised ed., Cambridge, Mass.: Belknap Press, 1974), 1:21–36.

Capt. Thomas Nairne's Journalls
to the Chicasaws *and* Talapoosies

Of the Government and Laws among the Ochessees and Talapoosies

To Landgrave Thomas Smith[1]

Talapoosies, January the 20th 1708

Sir, The Government of this people such as it is, seems to be the shadow of an Aristocracy, nothing can be farther from absolute monarchy. One can hardly perceive that they have a king, at all, for the Chiefs of Each Village whom themselves call Micho (and the Traders king) are only heads of small Townships, the largest wherof does not now consist of about 80 or 90 men.[2] Nothing more contemptable than the authority of these Chiefs. They seldom ever use any Coercion, only harrangue, if by that they can persuade it's well, if not they rarely inforce their orders by sanctions.[3]

Each town of the Ochessees tho not of 40 fameilies is a sort of petty republick, and hath all it's Officers within it selfe, first the Cheif then his Deputy, or assistant, whom they call Innehaw. He is the 2d person of the Village, receives all orders from the mouth of the Chief and carrys them about to the people. Next to him in order and honor are the Istechages, or councellers. This name in their Language signifies men well beloved, and is the most honorable name their Tongue affords.[4]

The Micho hardly determins any thing without consulting his Istechagoes, some ar of that order by birth (being the heads of such fameiles as first settled the society) others are such Considerable old officers, as are taken into that designly for their merit. Of these are more or less in every Town. The people themselves know and respect them, but it's imposible for a stranger to Distinguish them by their garb and Fashion, which in nothing Differs from the rest. All the honor they receive is either in Drinking Cacena, or at a publick feast, being on these occassions served next the Micho.[5]

The order of proceeding is never known or observed among them but By placeing of their seats in the Town house. Oposit to the Door a litle elevated above the rest is the seat of the Chiefs, where he, his brother and sons sit, next to him on his right hand are the seats of the councellers, and Chief warriors then of the other warriors. Opposit to them on the other side the house are seats for the populace and woman.[6]

The Chief and Istechagoes sons never enjoy their fathers place and dignity, but their sisters sons are taken into their Cabbins when young, hear their consultations, and are instructed in their customs that when it comes their Turne they may know how to rule The Town. Histories inform us of severall people among whom the sisters son succeeded, and the son of the last reigning prince particularly Tacitus of the Old Germans [and] Bed of the Picts a British Tribe, but of German Extract.[7]

A man cannot forbear smiling to see a Cheif and his Istechagoes sitting close laying their heads togather, looking very sage and whispering, as if upon some very weighty affair, when their consultation may be only about planting, howing or the like. After the business is resolved on it's scarce ever contradicted but put in Execution, for these rulers never venture to send out any orders but what they're sure will be obeyed.

If it hapen after the Chief, and his counsell have resolved on a point, and any of the Town refuse to comply, all the punishment they inflict is to say they are mad, and wont Listen to what is right. It makes the other people grumble against the refractory party For not submitting to the good orders and customs of the Town, which makes him ashamed and comply very peaceably.

All the Governing which the Town allows the Chief is
first howing his field of corn, giving him the first Dear and
Bare that is taken at every generall hunt, fat or lean he must
take it as it comes, for these honest men don't pretend that
their subjects should contribute too much, to mantain a
needless grandure. They are content to share with their people in assisting and setting them a good Example the better
and more patiently to endure the necessary toils of life.

When publick work is resolved on, as building planting or
the like, if any person absent himself above 2 days, the Chief
and Counsell send the warriors who Pillage his house of
such things as they can find, sell them and add to the Town
stock. For theft the punishment is to make restitution, be
reprimanded by the Chief and accounted infamous. This
among them has much more effect than Loss of life with us,
tho now it begins to be more practised than formerly, the
sight of English goods being a greater temtation.

In case of murther the next kinsman dispatches the
Criminal (at any convenient opportunity) without Tryall, or
formality this is allwayes allowed. For chance medly [sic;
melee?] a present is made to the kindred of the party slain,
by his fameily, who casually comitted the offence, they must
likewise put the first slave they take in his place, to make up
the number of the fameily.[8]

If a man kills his Brother (tho that is Extraordinarily seldom) their is no punishment inflicted, all that they'le say,
what can be done it was his own flesh, he was mad when he
did it, and will be sory enough when he comes to his right
sences. Their opinion is, that the Loss of so nigh a relation,
is punishment sufficent. For recovery of Debets, the Chief
does not concern himselfe with the matter but it's seldom
but they pay one another faithfully for he [is] reckond a
rediculous person and Dealing with him avoided, who does
not perform his ingagements. Indeed the Cocique harrangues
Vigorously to make them pay the English peoples debts,
and hold forth the Ill consequences naturly ensuing from
their not encourageing Trade by Just payments among

themselves. If the Debtor prove too Negligent the Creditor
only goes to his house and takes the value of his Debt in
what he can find. When a man dyes endebted to any of the
English Traders, it is the soonest paid of all other debts, for
they don't care to hear their dead kinsman so much as
named. If the relations can pay the debt with ease to
themselves they do so, if not the Village won't suffer them to
be reduced to too great extreamity but immediately contribute and Discharge it.[9]

I had 2 Daies agoe the opportunity of seing a Coronation
or what's answerable to it among the Tallapoosies. The Governor having sent a Commission for Cossitee (commonly
called the Ogfaskee Capt. because Chief of that Village) to
be head of all the Tallapoosies setlement, with a Blank Co-
mission for a Deputy.[10] He would not so much as touch the
Comissions, untill their should be a generall meeting that he
might be installed in his dignity, with these formalities
alwayes heretofore used by his nation in investing their
Chiefs with the Authority.

The seats being full of spectators, a fire and the Cacena
pots in the midle of the square, the head warriors took up
Cossitee first, and then his deputy, carryed them 4 Times
round the fire, most of the Company following in manner of
a procession, and singing or druming a sort of congratulatory
tone suitable (as they thought) to the occassion. I and the
English saluted the Chief and wished him Joy, so did all his
own subjects present, and then washed his head and face
with cold watter. I observed both Cossitee and his Deputy
shake and seem concerned. Enquiring the reason, was informed 'twas for fear of being bewitched, for the generall opinion of the Indians is, that men of power and authority are
generally the objects of the Vizards mallice, who frequently
bewitch them into lingering distempers. After this Inaugura-
tion the Chiefs neither Eate or slept during the remaining
part of the Day nor the night following for this watching
and fasting, they affirme, breaks all manner of spells, and
enchantments that may be formed against them and renders

them utterly ineffectuall; but to divert him from the thoughts of sleep, all the woman of the Village, danced untill it was day, and now and then an officer appointed came and washed his face with water.

Sir, This is what I have observed and Learned of their Government which tho mean, is much better than none at all. I shall some whate improve it, by getting them gradually, to introduce punishments. In the mean time I've ordered the 2d principle Chiefs to forbare goeing to hunt, but to go from Village to Vilage and excercise their oratory for the publick good and in putting to flight such Crimes as would disturb their Societys, promising to make them an allowance out of the present of skins, to recompense for the Loss of their hunting. I remain Sir Your humble Servant, Thomas Nairne.

An Account of the Customs, Humers, and Present State of the Chicasaws

To Ralph Izard Esquire for the use of
the Board of Comissioners[11]

Aprill the 12th 1708

Honored Sir, The Chicasaw Tribe at present consists of about 700 men Devided in 8 Villages, the Chief whereof is that of Hollatchatroe lying in the Latt: of 34 about 700 miles west from the Meridian of Charles Town, 80 miles East from the Banks of the Missisipi, 160 miles North from the French Fort Lewis or Mobile, 60 miles S: by west from the Nighest part of Cussate river. These Villages stand by Creeks which make the head of the Chacataw river and that is a Branch of Mobile River that Falls into the Bay of Spirito Santo, Navigable for Canoes within 15 miles of the Chicasaw Villages.[12]

They (as all others) came over the Missisipi from the N: West and cane give little more Account of their Originall but have been here a considerable time, nor are they mentioned in the Journal of Soto's Voyage, and they are the only peaple whome I have met with, who have any Tradition of these Spaniards being among them. Some old men here show the way they Entered and Departed out of their Nation with the Hill where they Encampt.[13]

There Freinds are all Indians subject to the Government of Carolina, and the Chacchumees and Yassaws, to the south west of them, are their Enemies and all others wher they can with the Greatest Ease, get a Booty, but have most bickering with the Chactaws who live 60 Miles south of them.[14] To these being unarmed the Chicasaws did great Damage but they begin now to have gunes plenty and are better able to defend themselfes. Formerly when the Iroquois troubled these parts, they Drove the Chicasaws out of their Towns and made great Havock of them, but haveing attempted the like since they were furnished with Gunes found so warm a reception, that they thought fitt never to return since, but they who Create most trouble to the Chicasaws are the Paywallies (or Illinoies) whom they call Currus.[15] These people are Cowardly, dare not fight or attempt Towns as our allies doe, but then [sic; they] are the slyest and most patient men stealers of the World, for they sculk close by the Towns untill they have done some Murther, and Fly off with all speed. They duely visit the Chicasaws once or Twice a year, some times get home safe and some times not. Nothing Endeared me more to the Chacasaws then the promising if all our designs hit here abouts, to raise an Armey and Deliver them from that Persecution. The reason these Paywallies have this advantage over them is because the Chicasaws are no Watter people, know nothing what belonges to Canoes, and the others liveing on a Bank of the great river, falls Down with the stream then Cross over Cussall [sic; Cussate] river and in some Creek hide there Canoes. When persued they take them and away, but the river stops the Chicasaws from further persuete. For this reason it is they have many old Accounts to score off with the Paywillies, when a fair opportunity Presents.

The Chicasaws are arrogant and conseited, high minded touchy as tinder a small matter puts them out of temper are great pretenders to Honor, and Cannot bear the least affront

of One another. This humor has been hightend, by their
success in the warr against their Bow and Arrow Neighbours,
for they chancing to procure a Trade with us, soon made
themselves terrible to those who wanted that advantage, so
they have now the reputation of the most military people of
any about the great river.

The Chicasaws are to the Talapoosies as men of Quality
among us are to the peasants, look much more brisk, airy
and full of Life and tho in the same garb yet their mien is
very distingushing. Add to that both sexes of the Chicasaws
are proper handsom people, exceeding the others but are
nothing near so Civellized, quiet and good Natured; much
less managable and subject to Government nothing so man-
nerly and Complesant as the Ochesses but more surely and
moross and far less adicted to dancing mirth and gallantry.

Each Village of the Chicasaws has a cheif, who are all in
some kind of subordination to him of Hallachehoe, which is
the mother-Town, but the Cheifs Authority is dwindled away
to nothing, his Power is contemned and the head Military
Officers carry all the sway. Enquiring into the reason of this
[I] was soon satisfied that the kings own mismanagment
brought his Authority to be Disregarded, and that engaging
himselfe in such Actions as were by the constitutions of their
Government contrary to the Duties of his place, for by Law
the kings power was Limetted to matters relating to peace.
He was not to be guilty of sheding the Least Blood, was to
opose all projects of Distroying, was Vigorously to harrangue
the Warriers, to keep firme to the Treaties of Peace with their
Freinds and Neighbours, was not so much as to be present at
the Execution of an enemy, and might save hime let the
desire of revenge be ever so great. In short his Duty obliged
him by all wayes and means to promote peace and quiet, and
to be a Counterpoise to the fury of the Warriors. He had
likewayes charge of the other concerns of the nations, (except
War) kept the woman to their Duty of making plenty of
Corn that their may be no want, but instead of this the present Chief Fattalamee, finding that the warriors had the best

time of it, that slave Catching was much more profitable
than formall harranguing, he then turned Warrior too, and
proved as good a man hunter as the best of them. But for
this infringing the Constitutions, the people don't regard him
as king, for it seems they're of the whiggish opinion that the
Duties of kings and people are reciprocall that, if he failes in
his they've sufficient cause to neglect their's.[16]

Tho the Chiefs Authority at the best be none of the
greatest, yet hees invested in't with something of Pomp.
When one dies, his sucessour (that is his sister's son) is put
in his place. The chiefs of the other Villages with their
assistance come to Hollatchahoe make a Bower, sing 3 Dayes
and nights.[17] An officer who waits without carryes them in
necessarys but no others see or disturb them. Dureing these
4 Dayes the warriors are bussied preparing a Cabin or chair
of state of white wood and rubbed over with Chalk to put
him in mind of peace. The 4th Day in the morning they
bring out the intended king and his son whome they place
on the Chair which the warriors lift with a shout and carry
to the Creek in a hole whereof the bearers plunge themselves
king and all three [times?] wash him well, and Returne with
him to his house.[18] The people in the road throw Corn stalks
on him to denote plenty, the rest of the Day is spent in
dancing. At night every one departs his own way. The party
is owned as Chief, and his son has a title of Honor given
him, denoting the 2d person, but does not think of suc-
ceeding. The heads of the Tygar, Muclesa, and raccoon
fameilys together with the Chiefs, do here make up the
Councell, that is about any affairs except these concerning
Warr.[19]

Their Laws about murther, theft and relateing to property
are the same as with the Ocheses. They put witches, Conjurers, and rain makers to Death by consent. Once that these
fellows have gained Great Esteem by their gulleries, they
begin to be Arrogant and strive to make every body Dread
and stand in Aw of them, by pretending to bewitch all their
oposers, or to hinder any rain from falling, and so sterve

them all. Upon hearing this one or another call's a Councell aquaints that such a person is an enemy to menkind, that will do so and so if not prevented, then they order one or 2 out of every fameily to wait and kill him that they all may have a hand in't. About 10 dayes agoe here were 2 killed only because 'twas a Cold backward spring which they had been ascribing to their own art. I am so far from being Angry with the Indians for dispatching such Rascalls that I think the punishment most just, not as they are conjurers, but impudent lyers, cheats and pretenders.

The Chicasaws Yassaws and other people of these parts have one pretty rationable Esteablishment that is that any fameily of a nation who pleases usually chuse a protector or Freind out of another fameily. He thus chose is generally some growing man of Esteem in the Warrs, they who chuse and owne him for the head or Chief of their Fameily, pay him severall little devoirs as visiting him with a present, upon their returnes from hunting saluting him by the name of Chief. Then he is to protect that Fameily and take care of it's concerns equally with those of his own. Thus likewise Two nations at peace, each chuse these protectors in the other, usually send them presents. His bussiness is to make up all Breaches between the 2 nations, to keep the pipes of peace by which at first they contracted Freindship, to devert the Warriors from any designe against the people they pro-tect, and Pacifie them by carrying them the Eagle pipe to smoak out of, and if after all, ar unable to oppose the stream, are to send the people private intellegence to provide for their own safty.

I can compair them to nothing in Europe, so much as the Cardinall Patrons in Rome only ones business is to preserve from Ware, the others from I know not what. The Chicasaws call thes protectors Fane Mingo or Squirrell king, and they are made after this manner.[20]

All or most of the Fameily come to the Village where the man lives whom they Design thus to Honor, their make an Arbour clear a peace of ground 30 or 40 yards square, on

this they draw a circle and Devide it with cross lines; by this
they set up an Eagle pipe looking due East. The Circle
signifies the sun which they think to be a proper Amblem to
represent Peace that Planet being so Beneficent and so
Freindly to mankind. Then they set 10 men and as many
woman a singing in the Bower 4 daies succesively from 2 A
Cloke in the afternoon untill 10 at Night. When they begin
to sing, a post is set up in the Midle of the square, by which
the warriors of the fameily dance War Dances, relate their exploits then give the post a Cut, with the Hatchett, and
throw Down some beads or something Else at the Foot of it,
which are Devided among the singers, and are a fee for their
Trouble. The 4th Day the Chief Elect is brought and placed
with his face to the sun riseing, the Warriors again Dance
the Warr Dances befor him, and Cut the Post so that at
Twelve a Clock it falls and this only to signifie that thus he
shall cut to peices all his Enimies. Then the Warriors dance
the peace dance 4 times round the square, with the Eagle
pipe carryed befor them, then the chief is washed and carryed to his house with the pipe of peace born befor him so
the ceremony Ends. At present the 3 Chief Military men
who carry all as they please are Chincoboy Micho, Oboystabee and the war king as they call him.[21] These arrived to
this Honor by the greatness of their Actions, and the respect
which all the soldiery bear to them, which has made them
all by consent, own them for their Chief Officers, and do
nothing in any Considerable Design but what is projected,
and led on by them, tho every private Capt. with his
Followers or every single man or 2 goe a free booting at their
pleasure. Tho the Chicasaws little regard the Civil power, yet
they very much respect the Military officers. When any
English goods are in the Town to tempt them the Fellows
only go muttering about, what no Design on foot what are
all the officers doeing, that no expedition is goeing forward.
Among them the Generals cook who is likewise his waiting
Gentleman, Is a very Honorable post and frequently succeeds
him, for his Master usually aquants him with his most

powerfull Amulets charmes, and songs to procure success. This is a great step towards his preferment which with the Love of the warriors exalts him to the highest post of military Honor.[22] When any design is resolved on by these three all the Capts. who have a mind to goe, ar sent for, are aquanted with the Designed Voyage, and intended methode of managment have 8 sticks given to them to denote the time of 4 Dayes to provide Floware, shoes Targets, four others to Physick.[23] Their comon methode of Encamping is in form of a crescent. The Chief officers Lodge in the Center, no body must light a fire, untill the Chief Officers have struck theirs, and Delivered some to their attendants, who have theire fires Just before the Camp. The very same doe the other Capts. and their attendants so that there are a line of Fires in the Front which are all sacreed, and never used for any Comon use not so much as to light a pipe. They never blow the Chief officers Fires, with their mouths or any thing else but fane them with an Eagles Wing and that with great congruity as they fancy, because goeing on a Design of conquest they should use the feathers of a Foull that has formerly had such success in his arrival [sic; aerial] pillageings.[24] After the Front Fires are made, the forces make their Fires and Encamp behind them as they please. When the forces March 2 or 3 Warriors who are the best Pilots, March befor the officers. When they streach themselves in a Line, to Encamp, the Officers don't sit Down untill their attendants, have made them a place, taken from them their Amulet bages, laid them on Red Targets in a Line befor the front fires. They have a great conciet in these Amulet bages, and Esteem them of wonderfull Efficacy to procure success and dasle the Eyes of their Enimies spies so that they shan't be discovered.[25] I was constantly inquiring the reason of these foolarys but can not give none except the Antiquity of the Custome, and the congruity of carrying parts of all destroying voracious creatures when goeing upon the like Designe. For in these bages are powders of strong Intoxecating roots, and some parts of all fierce kind of Foul and beasts, that live on prey. A small

Lock of Hair of every prissinor they take is alwaies put into
the amulets bages. When the hunters come in with meat
they lay it all Down a minute or 2 befor the amulet, and
then carry it back to dress. They throw by them likewise a
bit of meat out of every Dish in the Camp, which they say is
an offering to the spirits of such as are to be killed, and out
of every dish of Victualls in the camp, a little bit is thrown
into on of the sacred fires befor any of it be Eaten.

There ar 2 Millitary Orators that go every night through
the Camp and Harrangue courage into the soldiers.

The night before they expect to fall on, the Officers open
their amulet bages, and hang a litle about every sholdier's
neck. If it be a Village to be surprized, they place themselves
in form of a halfe moon, march towards it, when the Chief
Officers gives the signall with his whistle, every man Clapes
his hand to his mouth, gives the War Whoop, and then
catch as catch can. After an exploit is done, good store of
prissoners taken, and Danger a little over, they hang their
bages about their prissoners necks and set them all advanc-
ing, and that only to Honor the amulets, which in their notion hath procured them so good success.

The Chicasaws ussually carry 10 or Twelve Young woman
with them to the Warrs, whose bussiness is to sing a fine
Tune, dureing any action. If their own men succeed, they
praise them highly and Degrade the Enimy but if they give
Back the singers alter their praises into reproaches, Thus
changeing notes according as their party advance or give
way.[26] There methode of makeing men warriors is thus, the
Chief fameilys of one side must be made warriors by the
Heads of the other fameilys. No men by Doeing an exploit
becomes a warrior, untill that Honor be publickly bestowed
upon him, and a warrior must be a warrior of some fameily
but never of his own, and he may chuse which, thus suppose
A being a young man of the Dear fameily, kills an enemy
brings the hair (or else a prissinor) to some Chief man of the
Hauck fameily, that man is bound to see Honor done him,
to be his patron, and the other alwaies remains his, and his

Fameilys Warrior, and obays them in severall things. After
the Patron has recieved the hair or slave, he provides a present to return, calls the heads of the Fameilys together, who
consult of a proper war name, make 2 small white Arrows
call the person to be honored by his new war name, who
after the 3d call rises up, his patron presents him with the
arrows to stick in his hair, gives him a present, and every
one of that fameily gives some small thing. Likeways upon
doeing more or greater exploits, he has a higher name and 2
more Arrows given him, untill as great as their Titles of
Honor goe. The Ochessees and other warriors use these
small white featherd arrows likewise. No man ever presumes
to weare one unless thus publickly given, he would be a
comon redicule the same as if a tradsman in England should
wear a star or Garter. Tho the power of the Military Officers
be considerable when abroad, yet in the Towns in a time of
peace, every man almost thinks himselfe as good as another,
and only obeys so much of his superiors commands as suits
with his own convenency or humor.

It is a point of Honor among the Chicasaws to stay 4
Days in an enimies Country, for which reason they usually
staye 2 Intire dayes besides these upon which they went In
and came out.

The Chicasaw Customes relateing to woman are singulare
and much Diferent from the other Savages. They are far
from allowing them these scandelous libertys, which are usual
Else wher. They bring them up with more Decency and
reservedness, so that modesty becomes habituall to them. You
shall not see them ogle and splite Glances as the other
savages Ladys Usually doe. What ever their minds are the
Custom of their Country keeps them within due bounds of
Decorum. Hardly any such thing as whoreing used among
them. Neitheir is any thing more Odious and scandelous,
and that hatefull distemper frequent Else wher is not in their
whole Country.[27] This people are all togather for Impaling
[impeding] even their young wenches, or at lest the watchfull
Eye of their Aunts and mothers, carfully avoid makeing

themselves cheap by being common. When any of the
English Traders tempt the vertue of a young Chicasaw ladie
with a present, they usually reject it, with contempt, what
(say they) you think you're among the Ochesses now, how
brutall a proposall you make, a night thats the way that
beasts couple it belongs to mankind to be more particulare.
He that has me shall take incumbrances and all, and cohabit
after that sociall manner, which love and Freindship require
and if you incline to that you just aplay your selfe to my
Unckle and Mother, and they'le tell you farther.

The Chicasaws keep their wives, in good order, and
within due bounds, much after the same manner as honest
blind Milton advises in his Sampson Agonistes, never part
with the Masculine prerogative of ruleing.[28] Its rare to see a
man among them subject to Pettycoat Government, look on
themselves too brave Martiall men far enough above that
they scorn so much as occasionaly to court a woman but
alway's send their Freind.

A Girles Father has not the least hand or concern in
matching her, he is not so much as of the same fameily. The
mothers Brother does all, and to him a suiter makes his ap-
playcation, if he gives concent, the bussiness is done, for his
Interest is so great with his sister and her Children, that they
seldom go against, what is resolved on. After the unckles
concent is procured the spark sends his Freind with a pound
or 2 of small beads, these he Delivers to the Mother. She
sends for her Brothers and sons and hold a consultation in
from whether it shall be a match or not. If it be agreed
upon, the beads are devided among the Girles nighest famell
relations who are ordered to provide good store of Bread and
other Vitualls against such a Day, then sett. Of this they
send the man notice, who against the Day, invites his relations. Upon the time apointed, the Bride comes with a Dish
of vitualls, and her Troop of Famell kindred, following in the
same order. When they have Eat and discoursed untill weary,
the Bride and her she freinds Depart, to her house, but the
Bridsgroom does not follow till night.[29]

Poligamy is such in fashion among the Chicasaws, the
men of note have all 3 or 4 wives a peice, they ar so used to
this custom they would never endure to be other wayes.
They alledge its the only convenient way of marriage, and
the properest methode to keep a woman in a pleasant humor
(for they say) when Dunce proves peevish and pretendedly
indisposed, we presently leave her to digest, what makes her
uneasie, and retire to the lively good natured Pacalce [sic;
Pacalis?] who is Ever ready to receive us, with a Chearfull
Brow and open Armes.[30]

The Beautys are so engrossed, by the men of Action, by
great Warriors and expert hunters that ordinary Fellows who
are sloathfull and unfortunate, are obliged to take up with
very mean stuff. These shabroons[31] are the only refuge of the
Ladys something in years, or who have for their Ill humor,
been dismised by better husbands. Thus indulgent nature
always provides som releife even for the most unhappy.

Among the Europians, this haveing plurality of woman,
would be chargeable and inconvenient, for a thousand
apurtenances must first be procured befor a wife, but here
Inqutae [sic?], (tho young and of Quality)[32] thinks herself
compleatly adorned, when wrapt below the Navell with red
or blew stroods, her hair Oyled and trimed up, her Ears
hung with glass pendents, her neck and wrists encircled with
beads of the same Mettel, neither can any other Dress make
her apear more agreable or add the Least to native beauty. If
her husbands ability does afford Jacketts or blanketts 'ts well,
if not drest Buffaloe calf skines suply the defect.

Among the Chicasaws the mother in Law, seldom or ever
discourse with her daughters husband, it's reckoned imodest,
but his wives breatherin have the same Freindship, with him
as his own have. This was a custom so Deferent from the
Talapoosies, wher the mothers in Law rule all the fameily,
that nothing can be more.[33] All the reason the Chicasaws
give for it that its their paternall custom. Some crafty fellow I
suppose haveing been teised with the impertinances of his
Mother in Law, introduced this usage. When a mans wives

Disagree it does not in the least trouble him he only
threatens to Cashier them all if they continue to disturb his
repose.

It is among this people, the prerogative of the masculine
sex to divorce their wives. The woman are not allowed the
same privelage, and dare not upon any Account Leave their
husbands, yet when a Lady chances to be very uneasie, she'll
by sullen pouts or other methods of Female Management
order matters so that her husband will dismiss her and then
she is at liberty, but if he don't make publick proclamation
that he has freely let her goe, no other dare venture to take
her without runing the risque of their lives from his relations. If a Chicasaw Lady intends to Cuckold her husband,
she must use the utmost conduct and discration, for upon
the least Discovery Death Certainly Ensues, both to her and
the gallant for the husband and his kindred seldom ever put
up an afront of that nature, so that adultry here is scarce
ever comited. If Cuckold makeing were as Dangerous an
Enterprize in the great European cities, the Beaus would not
value themselves so much upon their performances of that
kind, for Loveing a whole skin so well as they doe, they
would let the Ladys who has old husbands Languish under
the misfortune rather than run so great a risque for their
releif. The Chicasaws are very Jealous of their woman. Its
reckoned the greatest afront In the world for one man to lay
his hand on anothers wives, and married woman never
dance with any man, except their husbands brother or his
Friend.

The Chicasaws live in an Excellent hunting country, both
for Larg dear, and other game, but the deficulty of carriage
makes their trade of less Value, but their is a remedy to be
had for this. Formerly when beavor was a comodity they sold
about 1200 skins a year but no imployment pleases the Chicasaws so well as slave Catching.[34] A lucky hitt at that
besides the Honor procures them a whole Estate at once, one
slave brings a Gun, ammunition, horse, hatchet, and a suit
of Cloathes, which would not be procured without much

tedious toil a hunting. They goe a man hunting to the Chic-
saws [sic; Choctaws], Down to the sea side along both sides
of the great river, and 150 miles beyond it.[35]

As to the Domestick way of liveing of the Chicasaws it's
much like to the Savanoh's. The men apply themselves to
the warr and hunting, supply their Houses plentifully with
meat, the woman plant and howe the Corn.[36] It's reckoned
beneath a man to touch a howe or bring a litle wood to the
fire, and the Ochesees are suficently rediculed among them
for their Indulgence to the fair sex, but especially such
Chicasaws as have Ochesees wives, never scap being well
rallied by others of their Country men, who occasionally
ramble that way. What say they have you been obedient to
your wife and mother in Law this morning. Pray go cary
home some wood they'le be out of humor Else. Swans
feathers are great ornaments among the Chicasaws. They are
taken out of ponds, with lights in the night.

Their notion of spirits, and the world to come, is the
same with the Ochesees, they imagin they shall make their
apearance there in all Military pomp and bravery. They do
not keep the busks as the Ochesees, but only make a great
generall Dance, when they Eat the first green Corn.[37]

When a Chicasaw dies, some of his Warriors, or others of
an opposit fameily to his own, come, put on all his fine
cloaths paint his face stick his arrows of honor in his hair,
and bury him under his own bed In the dwelling house,
then set up a post by his door like a maypole, paint it all
over with red lead, break his bow, tye it, and his arrows to
the post, which they adorn likewise with the rest of his
Military ornaments, and with plumes of white and red
feathers from top to botom, then bring out his wives, untye
their hair, take off their Braslets, and set them together with
his mother and sisters, round the foot of the post a crying.[38]
Every evenning and morning for 4 months, they take a set
time by the post, of an hour or 2 long. At the 4 Months
end the Warriors come, pull up the post, throw it away, and
eat a small Treat purposely provided for them. After this the

Ladies cry within doors, and that only occassionally, for the
remaning part of the year of their widdowhood, as upon a
visit received from some relation or the like. When the year
is expired the widdow is drest trimed and oyled by the sisters
of the deceased, and then at liberty for a 2d venture. If any
of their late husbands Bretheren or nigh kinsman have an inclination to them they're obliged to accept of their addreses,
not haveing by Law the Least liberty of refuseing. If the
party hath been killed in the warrs, the Ceremony is the
same, only when the post is taken up its carefuly Laid aside
with all its ornaments, untill some person of that nation who
killed him, be brought to suffer in reveng, who is taken and
bound at the same post. For a woman the post is only
adorned with white feathers, and a swans wing tyed a Top.
Men have every where the makeing of Laws, and have been
favourable to themselves. A Chicasaw is obliged to mourn
but 6 Months for his wife, and that with no set tunes only
by neglecting his dress and looking dejected. They afirm that
by the constitution of human bodys, a woman can better afford to cry, and live unmarried a year then a man can six
months. For a Chield or young person, the parents brothers
and sisters mourn 4 months. When a mans wife dies, if she
leave any sisters unmarried, they cant refuse him if he apply
himself to them.

Because this paper may possibly remain a record for time
to come, it will not be amiss to shew how Just a tittle we
have to the Chicasaws, and that by a method the most moderate and equitable that ever dominion was acquired over
any rude savage Nation. The first Europeans which the
Chicasaws saw were some of Lesalles men, who came to their
Towns with some Savanochs, but they were so far from pretending to get any superiority over others, that themselves
were poor ramblers and they and a few Savanochs, thankful-
ly accepted of some feilds from the Chicasaws, to plant, and
stayed 2 or 3 years under their protection.[39] After this some
Savanochs perswaded 3 or 4 of the head men of the Chicasaws to go see the French Fort at the Illinois. This they did

once, but the Illinois happened to kill 1 or 2 of them. They
never went again.[40] When Doctor Woodward about 20 years
agoe made peace with the Ochesees and Tallapoosies these
people haveing then Freindship with the Chicasaws he sent
two of his men hither, who brought them aquanted with the
English.[41] Ever since, they have traded with Carolina, paid
their submission to this Government, without any knowledge
of or interruption from the French, untill a litle before the
proclamation of this warr, Monsieur Tonti came here and in-
sinuated into their favour by great promises.[42] It was not
honest for the French to endeavour to seduce our subjects
from their duty, in times of peace, but peace or war, they
generaly persue their own ends. It may be we are now at
Leasure to call them to an Account for it.

I shall conclude this Account with this observation that
the present Interest of Carolina in relation to this people is
to keep as good a Trade goeing in their Towns as possible,
have good intelegence of all transactions, make use of them,
In subduing or helping to bring over all others now under
the French, to conive a litle at the roughness of their temper
untill by degrees we bring them to be more pliable and that
their own help. If this Tribe were politicians, independants by
triming between the French and us, while as yet our power
in these parts is something nigh a Ballance but they're easily
perswaded to asist in all our projects, and themselves, must
then be subjects of course, when we have put the French out
of any capacity to raise an Indian Army.

Sir, the Chicasaw Country lyes so, among branches and
Creeks of the Missisipi, that there ar nigh it multitudes of
Beavor Dams. We have a great handle to enrich ourselves, by
the Beavor Trade, if your board can possibly revive it. It
seemes strange that if it's no comodity in England, that it
cannot be sent else where. I shall in due time (God willing)
demonstrate that we can easiely ruin Mobile meerly by purchasing Beavor skines, for their Dependance and suport is
from that Trade which they have from the heads of the branches of the Missisipi, which I shall I hope drive them away

from, if after we have conquered the people we cane purchase their comodities, and therby continue them in Obedience.

Sir, I have from hence rode about to such branches of the great river as are usefull to answer our designs, and don't talk by gaess. This makes me earnestly urge You to study all means whereby, their may be added to Carolina so profitable and inexhaustable a fund of Trade and which tends so much to our safty to Encourage. I am worthy, Sir, Your Most humble Servant, Thomas Nairne.

[Untitled Letter]

To Mr. Robert Fenwick[43]

Chicasaws, Aprill the 13th 1708

Sir, Designing for the Chicasaws I set out from the ochessees with Mr. Welch, on Tuesday February the 25th crossed over Cusa or the main branch of Mobile river. Our Company consisted only of 10 Chicasaws 16 Tallapoosies, whom the Chiefs appointed for my guard and to carry my goods and 25 Apalachys that were burtherners for my Fellow Traveler, who was goeing a Trading. Being thus strong we went the streightest road, tho it Lay along close by the Chacta Country, in some places not above 40 or 50 miles from their Towns, yet we rather chose to venture the Danger than go any of the other roundabout wayes which being safer are therefor more frequented. We had in our gang likewise severall woman for the savages also Esteeming them necessary troubles seldom Travell without some of them. Among these was a young Chicasaw princess who was carrying from the English setlement 2 young catts, to her country as a great rarity.

Nothing more contrary to my inclination, than being obliged to travell so slowly, and wait the pace of the Carriors. To make the time slide on as inperceivable as possible I diverted my selfe, by accompanying the hunters at their sports, for the Chicasaws are such excellent forresters, they never mist supplying the Camp with meat enough, and so civall with all, that what ever was killed they threw down to us, that we might order the devission as we pleased. Our camp was not much unlike a crew of Gipsies, only that we were all armed men. As we set out every morning, some quallity of the Chicasaws, who thought themselves too good to cary burthens marched at a Distance from us on both sides of the path to provide wher withall we should sup, and usually came all to the place appointed well Loaden.

We pitched camp allwayes about 2 or 3 a Clock (that any stranger [sic; straggler?] might have time to come up) then the Ladies went to making Broath or roasting Turkeys or what else we had. When the camp was placed the usuall divertion of the hunters was either to look for Bare, fire a ring for Dear or go to the Clay pitts and shoot Buffeloes, for you must observe that in the spring and all sumer, these cattle eat abundance of Clay. They find out such places as are saltish, which they like up in such quantities as if some hundreds of thousands of Bricks had been made out of them, and the paths leading to these holes ar as many and well Trod, as these to the greatest Cowpens in Carolina.[44] Tho our [sic; now] Buffeloe Bulls are not fitt for men to eat, yet in May, June and Jully the Buffeloe Bulls are very fatt and good, the Cows and heifers in the fall and winter. The tongues of these Creatures are extraordinary fine atasting like marrow, and that causes the death of many hundreds of them. Of all hunting deversions, I took most pleasure in fireing rings for in that we never missed 7 or 10 Dear.[45] Three or 4 hours after the ring is fired, of 4 or 5 miles circumferance, the hunters post themselves within as nigh the flame and smoak as they can endure. The fire on each side burns in toward the center and thither the Dear gather from all parts to avoid it, but striving to shun a Death which they might often Escape, by a violent spring, they fall into a Certain one from the Bullets of the hunters who drawing nigher together, as the circle grows less, find an easy pray of the impounded dear, tho seldom kill all for some who find a place wher the Flame is less Violent, Jump out. This sport is the more certain the longer the grownd has been unburned. If it has not for 2 or 3 years there are so many dry leaves grass

and Trash, that few Creatures within escape, and the men are
forced to go out betimes at some slack place to the leeward.
In killing Buffeloes they Aim at the yearlings and heifers, being the tenderest and indeed no Beef exceeds them. After
shooting 3 or 4 of these, no remonstrances can prevail with
the savages to march farther that day, but the Ketles and
spits to work. Sir, A hasty man can worst of any Travell in
Company with them, their whole discourse is, here's excellent grownd for bears or Turkeys, in this canepeice we shall
surely meet with Buffaloes, and 'twold in their oppinion be
perfect folly to pass by without hunting them. The heads of
you Brittans have in them a 1000 projects and chimeras,
about makeing yourselves great, rich, and the Lord knows
what, this keeps you perpetually in a hurry, which the more
prudent savages avoid by making happiness consist in a few
things. They're in the highest felicity when after a prosperous
mornings hunt, they sit with their mistresses, by some prety
Brook under the shady trees, enjoying the Fruits of their
Labour. When ther belleys were full one or another usually
entertained the Company with a song and his Ratle, and at
nights when it is the most danger, (to show the Chactaws
how little we vallued them) we used to pass away the time by
sitting up a Drum and setting our fingers and Dancers to
work, and because I designed to promote peace, I was usually
entertained with the songs belonging to the pipe of peace,
which are severall and the best the Chicasaws have. But after
our mirth was over we alwayes took care to lye with our
gunes and pistolls ready by our side in case of a sudden
assault from any party in the night, for the Chactaws often
beat up the quarters and kill Travellers in this path.

Upon a night alarm in the woods, the common methode
is to take your Armes, presently fly off from the fires and
wait the Issue. If the Enemy advances toward the fire, then
have the others a sure shot at them by the light of the fires.

About mideway a little on one side of the road is a
perfect salt spring, wher are to be seen multitudes of Buffeloes allwayes striving for it. I saw sea Coall in severall places

of this road, which is a rarity (tho of no vallue) in these parts of the world. I observed the more westward I went the more the Country was subject to Hurrycanes, for betwixt The Obechas [Abihkas] and Chicasaws, are severall peices of Land laid quite levell, some so lately that were yet with Deficulty passable by reason of the Trees fallen, others Cleared by the fire, they generally run in a Line from N:west to S:east 3 or 4 miles over 100ds Long. I saw beavor dams and houses. This is the most witty creature in the world. They talk of beasts haveing only Instinct, I wish all people had as much instinct for their owne affairs as this ingenuous Animall has.

If then the savages of our Company were cloy'd with dear and Buffeloe, then they went a Bare hunting. This was the time of year in which these Creatures lye in their holes, for from the first of January to the midle of March they sleep and neither eat or Drink. The Indian way of hunting them dureing that time, is only looking in holes under the roots of fallen trees, or up such trees in the swamps, which have a hollow rotten place nigh the Top. In these Large holes the Bears make their nests and repose themselves dureing their sleeping season. The savages when they spy such a hole in a tree presently view it all round and see for the marks of the Bears Claws in going up, thereby looking narrowly are easily seen. They either climb up some small tree that stands by together and prick him out with canes, or else fire the nest, as they come out of the hole, stand ready to shoot him. Thus I saw them take severall. After the Bare is skind, appears nothing but a mear coat of fatt 2 or 3 Inches thick which they likeways stripe him of, and this coat of Clear fatt will sometimes weigh 60, 70, or 80 lbs. but they are not so fatt Within as Hoges. They breed but once in 2 years, have one, two and never above 3 Cubs, at a time. Every 2d or 3 year all the woods here abouts swarm with these Creatures. They come hither from the Northern parts, when nutes are scarce there, and asoon as are grown fatt the strangers return to the place whence they came, and leav behind them only the natives of the place. The greatest obligation an Indian can lay upon his wife and mother in law is to carry home good store of this fatt to keep house with. They make bags of Dear skines and carry home full. The hunting law of the Chicasaws is, that who ever first finds the Bear, has the skin and Belley peice of fatt, and when driving a swamp he who first wounds him, has the same advantage. The rest of the fatt and meat are equally devided among the fires. Of no other meat they make devission as not worth it, each takes what he will. I could never eat so heartily of this as of Dear, or Buffeloe, yet 'twas meer prejudice, for this Creature seldom preys on any thing, is cleanly, and eats generally grass and grownd nuts Acorns and chesnuts. The Chicasaws are so civil even among themselves that they allwayes present the Breast of Bear (being the best) to the most honorable fire in the Company. Accordingly, good store fell to my share. The savages in the woods sort themselves 7 or 8 to a fire accord-ing as they have more or less acquantance or respect for one another. Those who lodge not 40 yard asunder will come very formally invite one another to there fires to eat, tho they're (it may be) Doeing nothing else at their own.

On going from Cusa to the Chicasaws the rivers which we pass are the 2 Branches of Pedegoe and heads of Chactaw river, or the Creeks belonging to one or other of them all which belong from the large river Mobile that falls into the Bay of Spirito Santo.[46] I had in this Journey opportunitys of seeing all the methode which the Indians use in transporting themselves and goods. I thought nothing of rafts made of Dry wood or canes, of small Bark canoes, these were com-mon, but to see every man make a Boat of his bed, and therein carry over Cloaths Arms and Ammunition very dry, was a thing I had not seen before. They take a Bare skine, or large raw buck skine, without holes (or these sowed up,) this they lay up at the four corners and therein place any thing of 50, 60 or 100 weight, their Gun fastned on Top of all, which they hold by the end, and therewith push the boat

before them themselves swimming after. Thus they transport
Powder Broad Cloth or any other goods without takeing the
least wett.

At Leasure in the way I learned of Oboystabee (whom
you made so much of in Charles Town) and who is Chief
Warrior of the Chicasaws, the inclination of the Leading men
and all other of his people relating to their Alegiance to our
Government which the French of Mobile, by presents and
promises so much shook of late. Sir I must (by the way) in-
forme you that the savages espeacially those so remote have
not a right notion of Alegiance and its being indefeasible.
They're apt to beleive themselves at Liberty, when they
please to turn to those who sell them the best pennyworths,
and tho the Traders take pains to instruct them, and by good
arguments endeavour to draw them from that Erronious doc-
trine, yet nothing but a much beter trade and the reputation
of far greater Courage then the French could have kept this
Tribe in any tolerable subjection. These, with them, were
motives, much more powrfull then the Justice of our cause.

After this Gentlman had informed me of most things
materiall relateing to his Country, he thus went on. About 6
years agoe (say's he) Tonti with 7 or 8 Frenchmen more came
up to our Towns, through the Chicta Country, made peace
with us, and presented our Chief men very liberally, invited
us Down to their Fort, and in passing patched up a peace
betwixt us and the Chictaws.[47] To be free with you Capt.
said he I was one of them who was deluded, by their great
promises. They boyed us up with a mighty expectation, of
what vast profite we should reap by Freindship and commerce with them, so that upon their Desire I Killed one of
your subjects the Albamas and carryed them the hair. But
after suficent Tryall made, our people are now undeceived,
and are sory they should so lightly think of Trying new
Freinds, and do chearfully returne to their duty. It's True
(continued he) that 2 old men of some note go early [sic;
yearly?] down to the French, meerly for the sake of what
they can get of them, and they are so silly as to beleive these

2 cane do strange feats in bringing others over to their party, when it's not in their power. These 2 with few refuge[e] people who can neither hunt nor take slaves (and whome the French oblige with their Auls and needles) are all that have the least regard for them among us, but intirely in the English Entrest are every one of the officers and military men, for they dispose of their slaves to your Traders much to their advantage, and so doe the hunters their skines. Of t'other sex, the beauties and fine women who are the warriors wives and mistresses, are altogether of your party, for these ladies are so pleased to look sparkling in the dances, with the Cloaths bought from the English, that they would be very loath any difference should happen, least they again be reduced to their old wear of painted Buffeloe Calf skins.

About 20 miles before our arrival at the Towns the people met us, with Flowers and continued So to do in gangs, all the way to the Villages, the Warriors and Leading men giving us the whiff as their fashion is to wellcome their Freinds.[48] We lodged the last night of our Journey, on the edge of a swamp about a mile or 2 from the first Village, together with 50 or 60 Chicasaws who had met us. This they desired that there people might make provision to Receive us in form with the Eagle pipe next morning, but before midnight we all repented waiting for this peice of honor there falling a great storm of rain accompanyed with violent thunder and lightning.

About 20 miles from Cusa River, we led our horses over a Barren Rockey Hill from the Top whereof, we saw the Country all about and Back to the place whence they came. Most of the way continued to be miserable barren stony uneven land, untill I arrived within 20 miles of the Chicasaws, and then we had done with sand, stones and pines, the Country being pleasant open forests of oak chesnuts and hickerey so intermixt with savannas as if it were a made landskape. These savanas are not perfectly levell, like our's in Carolina, but full of gentle Ascents, which yet are not too steep for the plough, on the Top of these knowlls live the Chicasaws,

their houses a Gunn or pistole shot asunder, with their im-
proved ground peach and plum trees about them. The land
from hence to the Cicasaws their country west to the great
river and up it's Branches some hundred miles are all thus
intermixt with savannas, the fittest Country in the world to
sett up such a course of life as the present Turcamans or old
Nomades lived; remove from place to place and feed Flocks.
Thus happyly might the inhabitants of these Countrys have
lived, if they had not been infatuated to divide and rent
themselves into so many petty Tribes and by that means have
endless feuds and warres one with another. This makes it just
now come in my head, to observe to you that conquest is
neither at some times nor in all cases unjust, nor unhappy
for these conquered for it had been infinitely better for these
infedils, if some powerfull tribe had subdued the rest, and
brought them under government and to a peaceable life,
rather then they should thus have consumed themselves, by
their savage quarrells. Thus the Incas of Peru acqueired a Just
impire, by making War only against such as were notorious
breakers of the Law of nature, whom they brought to be a
great nation, liveing peaceable and happy.[49] Tho these parts
have been a little more populous then at present, yet have
never been thick stocked with inhabitants, and I think 'twas
impossible they should by a people liveing without religion,
law or useful Arts.

It's now that season of the year, when nature adorns the
Earth with a livery of verdant green, and there is some
pleasure in an Evening to ride up and down the savannas.
When among a Tuft of Oaks on a riseing knowll, in the
midst of a Large grassy plain, I revolve a thousand things
about the primitive life of men and think how finely on such
a small Hill the tents might stand and from thence men have
the agreeable sight of the Flocks feeding round them. Thus
lived and rambled the great Patriarch in the plains of the
East, thus stood the tents under and about the Oakes of
Mamre. In this state of life it was that the bright inhabitants

of the Regions above designed to decent and converse with men.

The Land here is a thinn mold on Topp of a red stiff Clay and white Marle. The Curiosity which I observed most was to see Oyster shells every where spread over the Old Fields and savanas, as plentifully as if it were on Island by the sea, espeacially on the declining sides of hills, where the rains had made gullys there were great beds of them, some deep, some nigher the surface, and thus it is not only here, but all over the Chactaw Country. The Chicasaws beat them to peices and mix them with clay to make Earthenware. Whither these shells be like unto those of the sea shore nighest to place where they lye, which is the bay of Spirito Santo, I cant tell, but they're remarkeable different, from ours in Carolina, are far larger the shells very much thicker, and a twirle at the end.[50] How they cam there is deficult to Account for, being by computation about 220 miles from the Sea. I enquired if any lakes or rivers farr or near yeilded any the like, but was satisfied there was none such. If they came by the Floud it's strange that their should non [sic; not] be seen all the way from our Country here which is 700 miles especially since nothing can be said of the high or Lowness of the land here, but may be said of other parts. Against their being of a spontaneous production of the Earth, or play of wanton nature, it may be urged that none are found intire or encreasing but all show signs of age and decay: tho some are very sound little broak and scarce perceaveable moldered so that may yet last many thousand years, but others are the quite contrary. If nature once produced these shells, why should not such seminall principalls still have the like Effect. It seams more easey to have recourse to some whirlings or Eddies of the Floud upon it's decrease.[51] About this country are more violent Lightnings and thunders than with us in Carolina which proceeds from the moist savanna Land, and great rivers. This setlment bears from Charles Town west 1/2 a point Northerly. I see no other fruets the Chicasaws have

except peaches; and plums, red, Blew, and yellow. Each house
hath by it a grove of these plum trees, for it seems they bear
best, when run up in thickets 4 or 5 foot asunder. Over all
the old Feilds are strawberrys innumerable and that good and
Large. The woman supplyed me with these and were well
pleased upon receiving 2 or 3 strings of small beads in
return.[52]

Tho we saw no Chactaws in the road yet some of their
hunters spyed us, and run home to tell they had seen a great
company of horse men (this was but 4) besides a multitude
of Indians. Sir the Indian spyes always multiply what they
see at a strange rate. Upon this news the Chactaws expected
a storm from the Chicasaws, which made them call in all
their hunters and look out sharp. I am worthy Sir Your most
humble Servant, Thomas Nairne.

An Account of the Names and Fameiles among the Indians together with a Hint of Their Native Government

To Ralph Izard Esquire

Chicasaws, Aprille the 15th 1708

Sir, It something pusled me befor I could thorowly compre-
hend how the saveges came to be this devided into divers
Tribes or nations of Diferent Languages, and haveing constant quarrells one with the other, yet at the same time pretending kindred, everywhere as far as our trade and Government reach. The Villages for the most part, consist of the
same names tho their Language be different. Upon the progression of one Tribe out of another, they have still retained
the same names but their Language and customs have been
much altered. The usuall names of their fameiles are the
Turkey, Tygare, dear, Bear, Eagle, hauck and bird fameily,
Lyslala or demedices, Ogilisa, muctesa [sic], fish etc.[53] Now if
a savage of the Tygare or Ogilisa fameily become a 1000 miles
off, and find any of the same name they own and treat him
as their kinsman even tho the 2 nations have wars together.
It is the easyest thing in the world, for an English Traveller

to procure kindred among the Indians, It's but taking a
mistress of such a name, and he has at once relations in each
Village, from Charles Town to the Missisipi, and if in travelling he acquants them with what fameily he is incorporated
into, those of that name treat, and wait on him as their
kinsman. There are some of our Countryman of such pru-
dence and forecast, that in case one family should fail them,
take care to make themselves akin to severall.

Among all the savages, it is Accounted the greatest crime
in the world, for a man to marry or Lye with a woman of
the same name tho never so remote or come from another
Country. It's very scandelous for them to be so much as
privately together. The same avertion we have to the worst
sort of Incest they have to that. Among the Talapoosies the
punishment is to be tyed and scratched all over with
Splinters of Turkey bones, which their own relations will not
fail to inflict.[54] But then thats only their own fameily. For
their wives, they never reckon affinity creats any such kindred, and they're so far from Accounting it Ill to have several
woman of the same house that it's accounted the decentest
thing in the world if a man will have 2 wives at once that
they be 2 sisters, or when his wife dies to take her sister or
next unmarried kinswooman. Establishing a Custome of not
marrying in the same name or family seems at first to have
been a politick contrivance to encrease Freindship and keep
peace.

The Savages reckon all their fameiles from the mothers
side, and have not the least regard who is their father thus if
a woman be of the Tygar or Turky fameily, her Childeren are
all so too. A princess has liberty of conscience to let whom
she pleases get the next heir, and not the Least reflection
against him or Barr to his succession.

It seems to be done with the greatest Judgment in the
world thus reckoning kindred from the womans side. They
are certain to be in the right, no interloping groom or
Coachman can never make a fraction in the line, or put
them out in their genealogy. They have demonstration in

their way, and we an uncertain presumtion. For this reason
the Chiefs sisters son alwaies succeeds and never his own.
The Indians call their Uncles and aunts, fathers and mothers
their Cuzons both of the first and second remove, Brothers
and Sisters.[55] The Grand mothers usually name the Childeren are often from some accident happening to the parents
about the time they wer born, thus if a man go abroad to
the wars when his wife is with Chield, he or the other will
give it a name betokening his success. The Girles names are
usually Flowar, Blosam, Doe, prety faun, or the like, the
mens are Valiant, strong, fortunate, hunter, Enemy etc.
They're no longer called by these names then [sic] they have
Done some Military Actions, upon which they have a ware
name and that is still changed to a more honorable, as they
perform greater feats.

When any person is taken prisinor and kept Long by an
enemy, and chances to make his escape, the first salutation
he has from his relations (who all gether round him upon his
arrivall) is to be entertained with a set tune of weeping.
When thats over they carry him 4 Times round the Fire
sprinkle ashes on his head, carry him into the river wash
him all over then eats by himselfe, 4 dayes takes phisick and
is again washed combed and oyled. All this purification is
because in their Esteem, he is rison from the dead, and come
to life again, for as soon as any person is taken, they Account him dead, and call killing and being taken prisoner by
the same name.

Sir that at once you may have a notion of the Indian
Government and the progression of on Village out of another, I'le Illustrate by an Example:

$$1 \quad \overline{\underline{\begin{array}{c} C \\ \hline \end{array}}} \quad 2$$
$$A \quad B \quad D \quad E$$

Suppose 1:2 to be a river, A: a populous flourishing Town on
the river side, straightned for planting ground. Upon some

disgust, or other reason 2 Leading men lead out Colonies of
30 or 40 fameiles Each and sattle 2 New Villages B: C:
Bechancing to florish and increase much, out of it by the
same means arise D and E. Now the Villages D and E will
respect A and all call it their grand father, B their father C
their Elder Brother, and these names continue by Tradition
to be given them. According to these relations they'le give
the Chiefs of these Villages respect and precidency in their
Town houses, but as for authority they look on their own
Village to be independent of all or either of them and free to
manage their affairs as best pleases themselves. When one
Village express the Deference which they owe to another
upon the account of seniority, their usuall expression is, our
fathers brought their first fires from thence. If the removeall
be but a small way, they continue one nation and manage
their matters in concert, but if by some quarrell a humor of
Rambling, or the like they remove a great way they by
degrees alter their Language and become another people.
Thus must have been the methode when encreased and
Emitted Collinies, but since the use of fire armes the fatell
small pox and other European distempers, came among them
they're obliged to break up their Townships and unite them
for want of inhabitants.[56]

In some Villages The Tygar in others the Turky or Eagle
fameily have the Cheifdom. Haveing thus plainly shewn, how
at first the savages societies came to be molded, I'lle take
liberty to insert an observation, these people liveing very free
under little restraint, their Nation small, It's probable their
Government may not be much unlike to those a litle after
the Floud. I took particular care to enquire and examine,
whither any thing like Patriachall power, was to be found out
of a single fameily, but if you please to note what I've Just
now wrote, about their never matching with woman of the
same name, youll perceive it to be imposible that ever so
small a society should be founded, any other way than by
agreement, that is a popular mans carrying out Collinies who

follow him either for some real or suposed Excellency. Now
he would never carry out his collony, as a Patriarch, for suppose his fameily be never so numerous and willing to obey
him, yet they could not inter marry. Thus suppose a savage
of the ogilisa fameily inclining to Erect a petty monarchy and
hath 50 men and as many woman of the same name, willing
to forward the project, he can never bring his designs to
perfection, unless he can procure as many Lyslalas or others
to accompany him, that according to their constant practice
the men of that fameily may take wives out of this, and the
woman of this, husband out of that, which cant be done
unless their fathers Brothers or the like carry them, and con-
sequantly never so small a society be formed but by consent
of a willing people. It's true after the Town is setled the head-
ship goes in a family out of respect to him who first kindled
the fire, as their phraises is. Whither this was the methode of
mens subdeviding themselves in the first ages I can't tell but
it seems not accompanyed with the tenth part of the difficul-
ties which the Patriarchall way involves it's favourers in, but
to put it more out of doubt, that the Indians Government is
a new human institution, and nothing of Patriarchship or
Jure Devino in the matter, the Chief's son never succeeds
nor a woman, tho her Children do both which will by noe
means consist with the Patriarchall scheme.

Plato nor no other writter of Politicks even of the most
republican principles, could never contrive a Government
where the equallity of mankind is more Justly observed than
here among the savages. Lilbourn certainly has been in
Amarica, or if not, might thence have been furnished with
excellent presidents.[57] He would have seen a prince, nobility,
and the Mobb all at work or play together, and so equally
dressed that an able Arithmetician could scarce have told
whose Cloths was of the most value, and the same in their
diet house and furniture. If this be not Compleat levelling, at
least in fact, I dont know what is, and in the very same
equall condition the other sex, the princesses ladies, and
comon Town Dolls, sitting makeing Basketts earthen ware,

playing or swiming in the River without any marks of Destinction, or once imagening her self too good to keep another Company.

Sir, since you have here had an Account of the fameilies and kindred of the Indians, it may not be improper, at the same time to aquant you with their freindship, for that subject is not very remote from the other. They are great pretenders to Freindship, even the boy and Girles have their freinds. Their freindships are of 3 sorts, men with men, woman with woman, and men with woman. They contract their Freindships with deliberation, and formality. When one person has an inclination to make another his Freind, and he likewise is so disposed, they defferr the ceremoniall untill both parties be equally provided with the necesary presents, and then the person who made the first advances, together with some of his relations, goes to his house whose Freindship he desires. After the Treat (which was purposly provided) is over, and the Company have discoursed of the benefits and conveniences of Freindship, the visiter and his kindred Deliver their presents, and receive from the other a returne of as great or greater value. Ever after this they are as much concerned in one anothers wellfair as Brothers. One must not marry the others sister or near kinswoman, for that would be incest. In there Esteem every person in the house where a man has a Freind are in his Intrest likewise.

I did not think to meet with any platonick love among the savages, yet nothing more comon than for men to enter into these Freindships with woman, both married and single, meerly for the delight they take in their witt and humor, but when a man has one of these she freinds he is reckoned in the same relation as her Brother, and offering at any scandalous familiarity would be accounted an equall crime as if it were to his sister. They may be together where and when they please. If any one offers to make remarks, and another informs that they are only 2 freinds discoursing, this immediately stops all censuring, yet, after all, some of the savages are so uncharitable as to say this refined familiarity is often made an Ill use off, and talk at the same rate as the Wagg Boccaline, does about the Vertuosi and Poesoses [*sic*; Poetesses].[58] Freinds never visit without a present tho never so small. The mens Freindships seldom disolve till death, the womans often do. In wars a man is bound in Honor to stand by his freind to the very last, to releive him out of Danger and bring off, if possible, [his friend] and this part they are generally very punctuall in performing.

Some times they only enter their Freindships, by riseing up and Dancing a Dance which they call a Freind dance at the end whereof they change Armes, cloathes and every thing about them, and this is the usuall method that they who are strangers use in contracting Freindships dureing their Travells, and seems to have been used by the ancient Jews by what is mentioned in the 1st of Samuel 18:4: Verse.[59] I remain Honoured Sir Your Most Humble Servant, Thomas Nairne.

Notes

1. Landgrave Thomas Smith was Speaker of the S.C. Commons House of Assembly in 1708 and one of the largest Indian traders in the province. His "Description of Pansecola, Mobile, and the Mississippi, February 22, 1719/20," in C.O.5:358, pp. 23–24, echoed Nairne's imperialist notions. See *Biographical Directory of the South Carolina House of Representatives*, 2:637–639; Brown, "Early Indian Trade," pp. 118–128.

2. See Nairne inset (frontispiece) and Robert Johnson to the Board of Trade, January 12, 1719/20, in H. Roy Merrens, ed., *The Colonial South Carolina Scene, Contemporary Views, 1697–1774* (Columbia: University of South Carolina Press, 1977), pp. 56–66, for information on Talapoosa and Ochese populations. In 1708 a group of Ocheses lived on the upper Ocmulgee River. They had migrated there from the Chattahoochee region during the previous twenty years and remained there until the Yemassee War. See Crane, *Southern Frontier*, pp. 36–37, 183.

3. The rank and duties of Creek *micos* are described in Hudson, *Southeastern Indians*, pp. 223–225, and in John R. Swanton, "Social Organization and Social Usages of the Indians of the Creek Confederacy," Smithsonian Institution, *42nd Annual Report of the Bureau of American Ethnology* (Washington: GPO, 1928), pp. 276–293.

4. Called *heniha* and *isti atcagagi*, these two ranks are recorded in Swanton, "Social Organization and Social Usages," pp. 285–300.

5. James Adair, *The History of the American Indians; Particularly those Nations adjoining to the Mississippi, East and West Florida, Georgia, South and North Carolina,*

and Virginia . . . (London: Edward and Charles Dilly, 1775), pp. 46–48, 108, 361. Adair's *History*, based upon his long career as a trader among the Chickasaws and Creeks, is an important source in English of ethnographical information on Southeastern Indians. See Robert M. Weir, "James Adair," in *Dictionary of Literary Biography, Volume 30, American Historians, 1607–1865*, ed. Clyde N. Wilson (Detroit: Gale Research, 1984), pp. 3–6; Charles Hudson, "James Adair as Anthropologist," *Ethnohistory* 24 (Fall 1977):311–328; and Wilcomb E. Washburn, "James Adair's 'Noble Savage,'" in *The Colonial Legacy: Volumes 3 and 4 in One, Historians of Nature and Man's Nature*, ed. Lawrence Leder (New York: Harper and Row, 1973), pp. 91–120, for assessments of Adair's *History*. On cassina drinking, much of which is based on Adair, see Swanton, "Religious Beliefs and Medical Practices of the Creek Indians," BAE, *42nd Annual Report*, pp. 536–544; William L. Merrill, "The Beloved Tree: *Ilex vomitoria* among the Indians of the Southeast and Adjacent Regions," in *Black Drink, A Native American Tea*, ed. Charles Hudson (Athens: University of Georgia Press, 1979), pp. 40–82.

6. Adair, *History*, pp. 421–422; Hudson, *Southeastern Indians*, pp. 218–220; Swanton, "Social Organization and Social Usages," pp. 197–200.

7. Cornelius Tacitus, *The Annales of Tacitus, The Description of Germanie*, trans. by Richard Greneway (London: A. Hatfield, 1622), pp. 264, 271; Venerable Bede, *The History of the Church of England* (St. Omer's: John Heigham, 1626), p. 77. See Hudson, *Southeastern Indians*, pp. 185–193, for a discussion of matrilineal kinship among Southeastern Muskhogean tribes.

8. Retaliation was the basis of most Indian tribal law. Adair, *History*, pp. 150–152, 380; Hudson, *Southeastern Indians*, pp. 229–232; Swanton, "Social Organization and Social Usages," pp. 339–341; John P. Reid, *A Law of Blood: Primitive Law of the Cherokee Nations* (New York: University of New York Press, 1970), pp. 63–71, 73–75.

9. Haan, "The 'Trade Do's Not Flourish as Formerly,'" pp. 341–358. See Swanton, "Social and Religious Beliefs," p. 187, on name avoidance.

10. Nairne probably observed this ceremony at "Ogfaskee," the chief town of the northern Talapoosas, north of the Coosa-Tallapoosa confluence, on the west bank of the Tallapoosa River. Cossitee's "coronation" was an adaptation of an Indian ceremony to the purposes of Anglo-Indian diplomacy. Nairne sought to reinforce the hierarchical powers of Creek head chiefs over village *micos* to centralize Creek political authority.

11. Ralph Izard was president of Carolina's Board of Commissioners of the Indian Trade. *Biographical Directory*, 2:357–358.

12. The eight Chickasaw towns and the French Fort Louis de la Louisiane (Old Mobile) are located on Nairne's map and on map 3 herein. For other renderings of the name of "Hollachatroe" and the names of the seven other Chickasaw towns see Swanton, "Social and Religious Beliefs and Usages of the Chickasaw Indians," *44th Annual Report of the BAE* (Washington: GPO, 1928), p. 212, and Vicenzo Coronelli, [Map of the Mississippi Valley, *ca.* 1684], ms. map in Beinecke Rare Book Room, Yale University, New Haven, Conn., published as plate 10 in

Barbara McCorkle, *America Emergent. An Exhibition of Maps and Atlases in Honor of Alexander O. Vietor* (New Haven: Yale University Press, 1985). Archaeological sites corresponding to Nairne's eight towns are located in the Chickasaw "Big Town" region on the south side of King's Creek, northwest of Tupelo, Miss. Jesse D. Jennings, "Chickasaw and Earlier Indian Cultures of Northeast Mississippi," *Journal of Mississippi History* 3 (July 1941):155–226; Don Martini, "The Search for Ackia," *Northeast Mississippi Historical Journal* 5 (November 1972):17–31; James R. Atkinson, "The Ackia and Ougoula Tchetoka Chickasaw Village Locations in 1736 during the French-Chickasaw War," *Mississippi Archaeology* 20 (June 1985):53–72; James Donald Merrit, "Trade Goods at Chickasaw Village," (1975), an unpublished ms. on file at Natchez Trace Parkway, National Park Service, Tupelo, Miss. Atkinson has unraveled much of the complexity of Chickasaw sites in the Tupelo area and has identified "Hollachatroe" as Miss. archaeological site MLe14.

13. The internal inconsistency at this point suggests a copyist's error. Two accounts of De Soto's 1540 journey to the Chickasaws were available to Nairne in 1708. See [Gentleman of Elvas], *Virginia Richly Valued . . . Out of the Four Yeeres Continuall Travell and Discoverie, of . . . Don Fernando* [sic] *de Soto* (London: Felix Kynaston, 1609), pp. 79–86, and Garcilaso de la Vega, El Inca, *La Florida del Ynca. Historia del Adelantado Hernando de Soto* (Lisbon: P. Crasbeek, 1605), Book III, Chapters 35–39. See Swanton, "Social and Religious Beliefs and Usages," pp. 174–180, and Adair, *History*, pp. 194–195, for a migration legend of the Chickasaws. See also Richard A. Weinstein, "Some New Thoughts on the De Soto Expedition through Western Mississippi," *Mississippi Archaeology* 20 (1985):2–24.

14. Nairne placed the "Yassaws," the Yazoos, on the east bank of the Mississippi River. See map 3 and frontispiece for the Yazoo and Chakchiumas. See also James A. Ford, "Analysis of Indian Village Site Collections from Louisiana and Mississippi," Louisiana Geological Survey, *Anthropological Study Number Two* (New Orleans: La. Department of Conservation, 1936), pp. 36, 98, 152.

15. See Nairne's map (frontispiece) for his placement of the Illinois. The term "Paywallies" corresponds to the Shawnee term "pewale," ascribed to the Peoria Indians, an Illinois tribe. See Bruce Trigger, ed., *Handbook of North American Indians, Volume 15, Northeast* (Washington: Smithsonian Institution, 1978), p. 680, and Jacques Bellin, *Remarques Sur La Carte de l'Amerique Septentrionale entre le 28e & le 72e degré de Latitude, avec une Description Géographique de ces Partes* (Paris: Didot, 1755), p. 120. Chickasaw-Illinois hostilities are recorded in "Letter of J.F. Buisson St. Cosme (1699)," in John G. Shea, ed., *Early Voyages Up and Down the Mississippi, by Cavelier, St. Cosme, Le Sueur, Gravier, and Guignas* (Albany, N.Y.: Cramoisy Press, 1861), pp. 60–61, 66, and Sieur Bienville and Salmon to Maurepas, April 8, 1734, in Archives Nationales de France, Paris, Ministerie des Colonies, Series C13A, Correspondence General de Louisiane, tome 18, f. 86, printed in *Mississippi Provincial Archives: French Dominion*, 3:666. See also Adair, *History*, pp. 411–412.

16. See introduction for a discussion of Nairne's revealing comments on "whiggish opinions" and also Adair, *History*, pp. 427–431.

17. Nairne's description of Hollachatroe as the mother town of the Chickasaws contradicts Adair's statement that in 1720 Chooka Phraa was the head town. Adair, *History*, p. 378.

18. The frequent use of the number 4 makes it apparent that it had some significance for the Chickasaws. See Arrell M. Gibson, "Chickasaw Ethnography: An Ethnohistorical Reconstruction," *Ethnohistory* 18 (Spring 1971):102, 104–105.

19. Here Nairne recorded the names of eleven Muskhogean clan names. According to Nairne the Tiger, Muklesa, and Raccoon were peace clans among the Chickasaws. His other list was a combination of Ochese, Talapoosa, and Chickasaw names, without distinction. They are: Turkey, Deer, Bear, Tiger, Muklesa, Raccoon, Eagle, Hawk or Bird, Lyslala or Demedices, Ogilisa, and fish. See Swanton, "Social and Religious Beliefs and Usages of the Chickasaw Indians," pp. 191–199, and Swanton, "Social Organization and Social Usages of the Indians of the Creek Confederacy," pp. 114–127, especially the table of clan names on pp. 115–116.

20. Compare Nairne's description of the installation of a *fane mingo* with the calumet ceremony recorded by Andre Penicault in 1699. [André Penicault], *Fleur de Lys and Calumet, Being the Penicault Narrative of French Adventure in Louisiana*, ed. Richebourg G. McWilliams (Baton Rouge: Louisiana State University Press, 1953), pp. 5–7. The ceremony Penicault described cemented a peace between Pierre Le Moyne, Sieur d'Iberville, and representatives of several Indian tribes, including the Chickasaws.

21. Oboystabee accompanied Thomas Welch to Charles Town in October 1707, where he was called the "Chickasaw General." Alexander S. Salley, ed., *Journal of the Commons House of Assembly of South Carolina, October 22, 1707–February 12, 1707/8* (Columbia: S.C. Historical Commission, 1941), pp. 4, 13, 24–25.

22. Called *tishomingos*, this rank is described in Swanton, "Social and Religious Beliefs and Usages," pp. 214–216; Gibson, "Chickasaw Ethnography," p. 111; Adair, *History*, pp. 166, 382.

23. For the use of sticks to record time see Swanton, "Social and Religious Beliefs and Usages," p. 246; Gibson, "Chickasaw Ethnography," p. 116; Adair, *History*, p. 75.

24. The sacred character of fire was a belief shared by all Southeastern Indians. See Swanton, "Indians of the Southeastern United States," p. 776; Swanton, "Social and Religious Beliefs and Usages," pp. 248–249; Adair, *History*, pp. 105–108.

25. William C. Sturtevant, "The Medicine Bundles and Busks of the Florida Seminole," *Florida Anthropologist* 7 (May 1954):31–70; Gibson, "Chickasaw Ethnography," pp. 106, 116; James H. Howard, "Some Chickasaw Fetishes," *Florida Anthropologist* 12 (June 1959):47–55.

26. Diron d'Artaguette to Maurepas, March 17, 1735, Archives Nationales,

Ministerie des Colonies, C13A, Correspondence General de Louisiane, tome 19, ff. 110–111, printed in *Mississippi Provincial Archives, French Dominion*, 1:245, records the presence of Chickasaw female exhorters in battle in 1734.

27. Adair, *History*, pp. 143–144; Gibson, "Chickasaw Ethnography," pp. 113–114.

28. John Milton, *Samson Agonistes, A Dramatic Poem* (London: Printed by J.M. for John Starkey, 1671), lines 1053–1060: "Therefore Gods Universal Law/ Gave to the man despotic power/Over his female in due awe,/Nor from the right to part an hour,/Smile she or lowre:/So shall he least confusion draw/On his whole life; not sway'd/By female usurpation, nor dismay'd."

29. Adair, *History*, pp. 138–141; Swanton, "Social and Religious Beliefs and Usages," pp. 225–228.

30. "Dunce" and "Pacalis" are likely literary allusions. "Lady Dunce" was a character in Thomas Otway's Restoration comedy *The Soldier's Fortune* (London: 1681). "Pacalis" is a Latin adjective meaning "peaceful." Adair observed that "the Indians . . . are so fond of variety, that they ridicule the white people, as a tribe of narrow-hearted, and dull constituted animals, for loving only one wife at a time." *History*, p. 139.

31. A disreputable person or ragamuffin, *ca*. 1700 usage. *Oxford English Dictionary* (1933 ed.), s.v. "Shabaroon."

32. Perhaps a copyist's error for "Jaquetta" or "Ingenue," a likely literary allusion.

33. Swanton, "Religious Beliefs and Medical Practices," p. 700.

34. Crane, *Southern Frontier*, Appendix A, p. 328, "Exports of Peltry, 1698–1765."

35. Almon W. Lauber, *Indian Slavery in Colonial Times within the Present Limits of the United States* (New York: Columbia University Press, 1913) and William R. Snell, "Indian Slavery in Colonial South Carolina, 1671–1795" (Ph.D. dissertation, University of Alabama, 1972) discuss the Carolina Indian slave trade. See also Donald Grinde, Jr., "Native American Slavery in the Southern Colonies," *The Indian Historian* 10 (Spring 1977):38–42, and Haan, "The 'Trade Do's Not Flourish as Formerly,'" p. 344.

36. A group of Shawnee Indians had settled on the Savannah River in the 1680s. Crane, *Southern Frontier*, pp. 19–20; Swanton, "Early History of the Creek Indians and their Neighbors," BAE *Bulletin 73* (Washington: GPO, 1922), pp. 317–320.

37. John Witthoft, "Green Corn Ceremonialism in the Eastern Woodlands," University of Michigan, *Occasional Contributions from the Museum of Anthropology Number 13* (Ann Arbor: University of Michigan Press, 1949), p. 53; Swanton, "Social and Religious Beliefs and Usages," pp. 248, 262; Hudson, *Southeastern Indians*, pp. 367–375. All rely upon Adair, *History*, pp. 99–111.

38. Jennings, "Chickasaw and Earlier Indian Cultures," pp. 193–196, 208; Hudson, *Southeastern Indians*, pp. 334–336.

39. This group may have been members of La Salle's 1682 expedition down the Mississippi River. *Dictionary of Canadian Biography*, 11 vols. to date (Toronto:

University of Toronto Press, 1966), vol. 1, s.v. "Rene-Robert, Cavelier de La Salle," by Celine Dupré; John D. Stubbs, Jr., "The Chickasaw Contact with the La Salle Expedition in 1682," in *La Salle and His Legacy*, pp. 41–48. Nairne's account may have been a Chickasaw version of the founding of Fort Prudhomme at Chickasaw Bluffs, Miss. See map 2.

40. The French version of this event differed considerably from Nairne's report. "Les trois Francois que j'avois envoyés de la Mobile, le 1er avril pour reconduire les Chicachas et les Chactas, et de là aller aux Illinois avec des Chicachas pour faire la paix, s'y sont rendus le 23 may avec cinque Chicachas qu'ils ont menés par terre. La paix est conclue et a resté entre eux." Iberville to Minister of Marine, February 15, 1703, in Pierre Margry, ed., *Découvertes et Etablissements des Français dans l'Ouest et dans le Sud de l'Amérique Septentrionale (1614–1754) Memoires et Documents Originaux recueillis et publies*, 6 vols. (Paris: D. Jouaust, 1876–1886), 4:629–630.

41. Henry Woodward visited the Creek tribes in 1685. Nairne's statement, if correct, is the earliest record of English contacts with the Chickasaws. Crane, *Southern Frontier*, pp. 34–36.

42. *Dictionary of Canadian Biography*, vol. 1, s.v. "Henri de Tonty," by E.B. Osler; Patricia Galloway, "Henri de Tonti du Village des Chacta, 1702; The Beginnings of the French Alliance," in *La Salle and His Legacy*, pp. 146–175.

43. Member of the Board of Commissioners of the Indian Trade. *Biographical Directory of the S.C. House of Representatives*, 2:246–247.

44. Nairne, *A Letter from South-Carolina*, p. 14; Mark Catesby, *The Natural History of Carolina, Florida, and the Bahama Islands*, 2 vols., (London: B. White, 1771), 1:iv–v; Mark Boyd, ed., "Diego Peña's Expedition to Apalachee and Apalachicola in 1716," *Florida Historical Quarterly* 28 (July 1949):15–20.

45. Hudson, *Southeastern Indians*, p. 276; Gregory A. Waselkov, "Evolution of Deer Hunting in the Eastern Woodlands," *Mid-Continental Journal of Archaeology* 3 (Spring 1978):15–34.

46. The two heads of the "Pedegoe" are the Black Warrior and Sipsey Rivers. The Chickasaw called the Tombigbee the "Choctaw" River, the route to the Choctaw nation. The Choctaws called the same river the "Chickasaw" River. In his 1755 map of the Southeast, John Mitchell recorded the name of the Black Warrior as the "Patagahatchee." Cumming, *Southeast in Early Maps*, plate 59.

47. Sieur d'Iberville recorded the Chickasaws' visit to Mobile in 1702. [Pierre Le Moyne, Sieur d'Iberville], *Iberville's Gulf Journals*, trans. and ed. Richebourg G. McWilliams (University: University of Alabama Press, 1981), pp. 171–175; Galloway, "Henri de Tonti," pp. 146–175.

48. "Gave us the whiff" means discharging firearms to greet visitors. See Henry Woodward, "Woodward's Westo Discovery, 1674," in Langdon Cheves, ed., *Collections of the South Carolina Historical Society, Volume 5* (Richmond, Va.: W.E. Jones, 1897), p. 459.

49. The notion of a *Pax Incaia* is found in José de Acosta, *The Naturall and Morall Historie of the East and West Indies* . . . (London: V. Sims, 1604) first published in Latin in 1588 with numerous French and Spanish editions during

the sixteenth and seventeenth centuries, and in Garcilaso de la Vega, El Inca, *The Royal Commentaries of Peru, In Two Parts* . . . (London: M. Flesher, 1688), which also had several French and Spanish editions during the seventeenth century.

50. Galloway, "Henri de Tonti," pp. 153–155; Adair, *History*, p. 358.

51. Tonti, reporting the occurrence of these shells, posited their origins as part of the great flood. His and Nairne's account may have been derived from the Chickasaws. Adair also commented on their flood-borne origins. *History*, p. 358; Galloway, "Henri de Tonti," pp. 164–165, 171.

52. Adair, *History*, pp. 359–360, 409–410.

53. Swanton, "Social and Religious Beliefs," pp. 190–215, with clan names on pp. 190–199. See also text note 19 herein.

54. Among the Creeks this punishment was meted out for adultery. Swanton, "Social Organization and Social Usages," pp. 354–355; Adair, *History*, p. 120.

55. See Fred Eggan, "Historical Changes in the Choctaw Kinship System," in *Essays in Social Anthropology and Ethnology* (Chicago: University of Chicago Department of Anthropology, 1975), pp. 71–90. See also note 19 for the effect of matrilineal descent upon a chief's succession.

56. Compare Nairne's discussion with Adair's on the demographic collapse of Chickasaw villages. Adair, *History*, pp. 353, 459–460.

57. A reference to Plato's *Republic*. John Lilburne (1614–1657) was leader of the republican Leveller movement during the English Civil War. *Dictionary of National Biography* (1949 ed.), s.v. "John Lilburne," by Charles H. Firth.

58. Trajano Boccalini, *I Ragguagli Di Parnasso: Or Advertisements from Parnassus: In Two Centuries* (London: Peter Parker, 1674), p. 22: "The inthroned Academians, contrary to their ancient Institutions, did some moneths since admit into their Academy the Vertuous Ladies *Victoria Colonna, Veronica Gambora, Laura Teracina*, and other famous Lady-Poets of *Parnassus;* which was done with so great applause of the *Vertuosi*, as the Academians, set on fire by the beauty of those Ladies, were not only very frequent at their Learned Exercises; but did every day publish such Poesie, as made the very Muses wonder: but it was not long e're his Majesty smelt a very displeasing savour; wherefore he commanded the chief of the Inthroned, by no means to admit any longer such like parties; for he had found at last, that Womens true Poetry consisted in their Needle and Spindle; and that the Learned Exercises of Women, together with the *Vertuosi*, was like the sporting and playing of Dogs, which after a while ends in getting upon one anothers backs."

59. "And Jonathan stript himself of the robe that was upon him, and gave it to David, and his garments, even to his sword, and to his bowe, and to his girdle."

Appendix

Thomas Nairne's Memorial
to Charles Spencer,
Earl of Sunderland

South Carolina, July 10th 1708

May it please Your Lordship,[1]
Having been Imployed by the Generall Assembly, of This
Province in the quality of an Agent, and Itenerary Justice,
among the Indians, Subject to our government among other
things usefull, to be known for the Safety, and Interest, of
this Colony, I aplyed my self, in particular, to have a very
minute account, of all people as well Europeans, as Salvages,
from Virginia to the mouth of the Mississippi. I have had a
personall View off most of These parts, Either formerly when
a Commander in the warrs, or This year by Travelling. Altho
my Inquiries & Searches of This kind are not Finished and
perfect, yett Considering, the Juncture, that peace must of
necessity in some small time be concluded, I could not dis-
pense with my self from Laying before your Lordship a map
of Such Travells & observations as I have already taken, to
the End your noble Lordship may at one View perceive what
part of the Continent we are now possest off, and what not,
and procure the articles of peace, to be formed in such a
manner that the English American Empire may not be un-
reasonably Crampt up. Your Lordships may depend on the
Inland Topography to be Exact as any Thing of That Kind,
can well be. The Numbers of The Inhabitant[s] I took with
The greatest Care.[2]

Your Lordship upon View of the Map will presently conclude that If the french now Setled at Mobile were possest of
all the Indians subject to the government of Carolina, and

had united them to Those of the Mississipi, they wold be in Circumstances to draw from among them such bodies of forces as wold be Intollerably Troublesom Either to the English Colonies or the Naked unarmed Country of New Mexico, and That this Province, only by trading and other mannagement can put a Check to Them. A Consequence of this is That This province being a frontier, both against The French and Spaniards, ought not to be Neglected.

I have represented this matter in such a true light to the generall Assembly, that They resolved to raise some forces, to reduce Either the French fort at Mobile, or at Least all the Indians Betwixt us and the Mississipi, now in their alliance. Accordingly I was Busy providing every thing for my voyage. I entertained Intelligence among the yassas, Tassas, and Nochess, Inviteing them to Setle up Cussate river.[3] I ventured my Life, and made peace with the Chactas. In short I designed to Incite by fair means all that wold accept of our friendship, upon the Terms of Subjecting themselves, to our government and removeing into our territory, and quite to ruine Such as wold not, soe that the french might never be in a Capacity to raise an Indian Army to Disturb us or our allies, & that the Lower parts of the Mississipi, being left Desolate, the trade of the uper might fall to this province by means of factories, Setled on Cussate river for the French from Mobile wold find it Extreme Difficult, to carry on that Commerce, unless had releif and defence, from the Indian towns, on the Lower parts. But as I was Imploying myself in Concerting measures for The Intended Expedition, The Intelligence of the french & Spaniards Designing to Invade Carolina put a full stop to it.[4] Only I continue to Invite over by fair means all that I can, which I hope will not be altogether In Vain. My Design was to fall down from the Talapoosies against the french with a fleet of Eighty Canoes manned with 500 Indians & 1000 By land 15 English on the one part and 30 with the other. With These forces I pretended Either to destroy or remove into our Territory all the

Salvages from Mobile to the Mississipi, & up the river to 36 Degrees of Latitude.

The French of Mobile have their Support by the furr trade from the head of the Mississipi & a good underhand trade with the Spaniards of La vera Cruz by way of Pansacola. That small garrison depends on Vera Cruz and Live in Extream good terms with Mobile being both afraid of our Subjects the Talapoosies who Last year burnt Pansacola town. Tho the French at Mobile be now weak yett they are well Scituated for Indian trade. I have fixed a red Cross to these places now Subject to Carolina and a Triangle at these in amity with Mobile.

May it Please Your Lordship the English trade for Cloath alwayes atracts and maintains the obedience and friendship of the Indians. They Effect them most who sell best cheap. This makes it necessary that the trade with them should in England lye under as small duties and Embarrassment as may be. Sixpence Custom for such dear skins as are small and not worth 12d. seems unreasonable.

Your Lordship may perceive by the map that the garrison of St. Augustine is by this warr Reduced to the bare walls their Catle and Indian towns all Consumed Either by us In our Invasion, of that place or by our Indian Subjects Since who in quest of Booty are now obliged to goe down as farr on the point of Florida as the firm land will permitt. They have drove the Floridians to the Islands of the Cape, have brought in and sold many Hundreds of them, and Dayly now Continue that Trade so that in some few years they'le Reduce these Barbarians to a farr less number. There is not one Indian Town betwixt Charles Town and Mowila Bay Except what are prickt, in the mapp, only am uncertain of the numbers of the Floridians.[5]

Our friend the Talapoosies and Chicasas Imploy themselves in making Slaves of such Indians about the Lower parts of the Mississipi as are now Subject to the french. The good prices The English Traders give them for slaves En-

courages them to this trade Extreamly and some men think
that it both serves to Lessen their numbers before the french
can arm them and it is a more Effectuall way of Civilising
and Instructing, Then all the Efforts used by the french
Missionaries.

May it please your Lordship the English in next Treaty of
Peace have Just reason to Insist upon the French quitting
that Settlement on the Bay of Mowila because they Setled it
in prejudice to and Dispight of the Just Title the English had
to that Bay and the Rivers of it. It Seem they found the
Mississipi unfitt to Setle on, and not willing to give any um-
brage at that time to the Spaniards by going to The westward of it, made bold (Tho in time of Peace) with the English of Carolina, and Setled on the bay of Mowila 150 miles
to the East of the Mississipi all the Inhabitants whereof had
for 10 years before Submitted themselves and Country to the
government of Carolina, and then actually Traded with us.
The french upon their first arrivall were so liberall of their
Presents that they Entirely decoyed the People of the Lower parts
from their duty and Endeavouring to doe the Same with
the Talapoosies that live Higher up 5 of them were killed in
the attempt as they were coming up by an Indian Called
Dearsfoot. This has made them desist ever since, and the
English are now in possession of the greatest part of the People of That River.[6]

Your Lordship by a view of the map will perceive that If
the English think fitt to use any Efforts to make themselves
masters of the furr trade from the head of the Mississipi, it
must be done by drawing up the Yassas &c to Setle on
Cussate river and making small forts to defend the Traders
merchantdise where the places are marked.

Your Lordship will likewise see that the Cherickee nation
now Entirely Subject to us are Extreamly well Scituate to
Keep of any Incursions which Either the Illinois or any other
french Indians may think of making into Carolina and in Effect So it is, they are now our only defence on the Back
parts But are themselves miserably harrassed by the Iroquis.

Your Lordship may please to write to the governours of
Maryland and New York to Interpose as much with the Iroquois in their behalf as possible.[7] All parts of the English
Dominions ought mutually to Espouse one anothers interest
in Every thing that relates to the Common defence against
the French and their party.

May it Please your Lordship I have Considered this Coast
what parts may be any way usefull to the Brittish nation in
order to Setle Colonies. It is Certain we have firm Possession
by means of our Indians, from Charles Town to Mowila Bay,
Excepting only the garrison of St. Augustine and the Island
of Cape Florida. If the English could spare people it Seems
fitter to Strengthen this Province then Setle any New, But If
an Inclination to Setle any Place to the East ward of the
Mississipi, Should prevaile, the old Country of the Apala-
chias is the only best, Being for 40 miles Long and 20 wide
Clear feild fitt for the plough, formerly mannured by the Indians who were four year agoe Subdued and the remaining
part of them removed to Carolina.[8] This place wold be proper for the Seat of a government to take in the Neck of
florida, and 100 miles to the westward along the Bay. That
Country is full of Catle and horses which before the war
Belonged to the Spaniard and Apalachia Indians but are now
all wild.

But if your Lordship please to have laid before you all the
Printed mapps, and Descriptions that are in England of the
Country to the westward of the Mississipi and Thoroughly
Consider all Circumstances you will Incline to beleive that
the English Nation can Setle a Colony no where to greater
purpose then upon some Convenient place any where 60 or
80 miles to the westward of the mouth of the Mississipi. It is
Certain there are Considerable numbers of Indians there, so
farr from being Subject, that are at Constant warrs with the
Spaniards of new Mexico. It is certain the French could not
persue La Salle's design formed against the mine Country, by
reason of their Present Circumstances with Spain, So that It
seems If the English put in and gett the Indians of Their

Side, it may be a means of at Least Enjoying a good Share of
the trade Both with the Spaniards and their Indian Subjects,
of that part of New Spain.[9] The example of Queriaso[?]
Shows us that neither galleys[,] men of warr nor garrisons
can prevent a trade of that nature and no man Can foretell
how favourable some revolutions of Time might prove, in af-
fording oppertunities worth Catching att, to gain Some of
the mines.[10] The Bay of Campeche Lying not farr of[f] the
Baymen might be Invited to Setle in the new Colony &
make it The port of Cutting Logwood from that port, above
all things arming the Indians, purchasing their Commodities[,] making Discoveries and sending Youths to Learn their
Language, to ship home their wood, from, and occasionally
Exercise the trade wold be of the utmost Consequence to the
firm Establishing the Colony for of them might be had men
ready at any time to help oppose the Spaniards. A thing of
this nature must be done with great Secrecy, and first Setled
with Considerable strength and fortified with the utmost
Celerity. If the Spaniard patiently suffer the French to goe
Sharers with them in the Peruvian trade Its equally Reason-
able that the English, should aim at gaining some of the
Mexican. Its easy to make the peace and Inland Discoveries
from Carolina, from whence we are already well acquainted
as farr as the Mississipi. 2 or 300 lbs. Sterlings worth of
goods proper will be Sufficient & for discovering the Coast
and finding a fitt River to Setle on a Sloop may be sent
from hence privately. I Remain Your Lordships most obedient
Humble Servant, Thomas Nairne.

[P.S.] Your Lordship I hope will please to pardon Defect of
Title whereof I am Ignorant.

[Endorsement:] So. Carolina. 10 July 1708. Mr. Tho[ma]s
Nairne with a Map and account of those parts.

Notes

1. *Dictionary of National Biography* (1949 ed.), s.v. "Charles Spencer, Third
Earl of Sunderland," by Gerard LeG. Norgate. Nairne emended this memorial
by changing several of the terms of address from plural to singular forms (eg.

Lordships to Lordship), which suggests that he originally intended the memorial to be sent to the Board of Trade.

2. See introduction for a discussion of Nairne's cartographic works.

3. This refers to Thomas Welch's visit to the lower Mississippi tribes *circa* May 1708. Welch suggested that these tribes move closer to the Tennessee River. See Thomas Welch's petition to the South Carolina Commons House, December 9, 1708 (cited in itinerary) and his petition to the Lords Proprietors, 4 December 1708, Nairne Mss.

4. *Journal of the Commons House of Assembly, October 22, 1707–February 12, 1707/8,* pp. 10–11, 33–34.

5. Nairne inset (frontispiece); Boyd and others, *Here They Once Stood, passim;* Charles W. Arnade, "The English Invasion of Florida, 1700–1706," *Florida Historical Quarterly* 41 (July 1962):29–37.

6. Crane, *Southern Frontier,* pp. 82–84.

7. For Iroquois-Cherokee warfare see David Corkran, *The Carolina Indian Frontier* (Columbia: University of South Carolina Press, 1970), pp. 9, 15.

8. In the aftermath of the 1704 Apalachee raids nearly 1,300 Apalachees migrated to Savannah Town, near Augusta, Ga. See Crane, *Southern Frontier,* p. 80.

9. Nairne refers to a reported plot by Dionisio de Peñalosa, a disgruntled official in New Spain, to hand over Mexico to La Salle and the French. See Nicholas de Freytas, *The Expedition of Don Diego De Penalosa, Governor of New Mexico, from Santa Fe to the River Mischipi and Quivira in 1662, as described by Father Nicholas de Freytas, O.S.F. With an Account of Penalosa's Project to aid the French to Conquer the Mining Country in Northern Mexico; and his Connection with Cavelier de La Salle,* trans. and ed. by John G. Shea (New York: J.G. Shea, 1882); Peter H. Wood, "La Salle: Discovery of a Lost Explorer," *American Historical Review* 89 (April 1984):313–317; Henry Folmer, *Franco-Spanish Rivalry in North America* (Glendale, Ca.: A.H. Clark, 1953), pp. 138–143; Jean Delanglez, "Penalosa's Expedition and La Salle," in *Some La Salle Journeys* (Chicago: Institute of Jesuit History, 1938), pp. 65–99.

10. A probable reference to Curaçao, in the Netherlands Antilles. In 1634 the Dutch captured Curaçao from the Spanish to establish a base from which to conduct an interloping trade with the Spanish Empire in America. J. Hartog, *Curaço, From Colonial Dependence to Autonomy* (Aruba, Netherlands Antilles: De Wit, 1968), pp. 43–60.

Bibliographical Essay

Thomas Nairne's *Journalls to the Chicasaws and Talapoosies* blazes two trails through the canebrakes of scholarly bibliography. In 1708 Nairne was a public official of South Carolina engaged upon a diplomatic mission to the Indian nations of the Southeast. His mission described in his *Journalls* and memorial of July 10, 1708 was an aspect of British strategic planning during Queen Anne's War. The diplomatic trail through the *Journalls* leads to traditional historical research methods and sources; that is, to the published and unpublished records of European and American colonial governments with forays into the private manuscript collections of prominent white men. There is another trail—the ethnohistorical one—that wends through Nairne's *Journalls*. Along this trail Nairne perceptively recorded the customs and social institutions of the Ochese, Talapoosa, and Chickasaw Indians whom he visited. This trail leads through the scholarly literature of anthropology, ethnohistory, and archaeology—unfamiliar terrain to this student of politics. Fortunately, Nairne provided helpful markers on this trail. Nairne recorded marriage customs, burial and mourning ceremonies, rituals of hunting and warfare, and scenes from domestic life but, because he was a politician—a natural relativist—he observed these institutions with an eye to the manner in which they demonstrated relations of political power. This enormous "bias" preserved him from the subtler biases of religion and aesthetics that mar the ethnohistorical records of other visitors in Indian society. The two dimensions of Nairne's *Journalls*—traditional historical and ethnohistorical— make the *Journalls* a good example of the kind of material Patricia K. Galloway discussed in "Dearth and Bias: Issues in the Editing of Ethnohistorical Materials," *Newsletter of the Association for Documentary Editing* 3 (May 1981):1–6. Galloway's essay describes her experiences as editor of Volumes 4 and 5 of *Mississippi Provincial Archives: French Dominion* (Baton Rouge: Louisiana State University Press, 1984).

Nairne's *Journalls to the Chicasaws and Talapoosies* is among the manuscripts of the British Library, accessioned as Additional Manuscript 42559. The British Library also houses manuscripts that relate to Nairne and the *Journalls*. Additional Manuscript 61623, the Blenheim Mss., contains items relating to Nairne's arrest in 1708 for treason and Additional Ms. 4064, the Sloane Mss., mentions the early scientific interests of Nairne and other South Carolinians. The Great Britain Public Record Office, London, houses the autograph manuscript of

Nairne's memorial of July 10, 1708 to Charles Spencer, Earl of Sunderland (Colonial Office 5: 382, no. 11) and many public records of Proprietary-era South Carolina.

The South Carolina Department of Archives and History, Columbia, is the repository of the public records of the province, colony, and state of South Carolina. These records include the Journals of the Commons House of Assembly and the journals of the Board of Commissioners of the Indian Trade, two bodies in which Nairne pursued his political career. Unfortunately, the records of the Board of Commissioners of the Indian Trade are lost for the years 1707 to 1710. Nairne helped found the Board and it is likely that the originals of his four letters, copies of which constitute the *Journalls*, were among those lost records. An array of recorded instruments—wills, inventories, deeds, and land grants—elucidate Nairne's economic and social standing. The South Carolina Archives also has microfilm copies of British Public Record Office materials that complement its holdings and enhance the Archives' value as a research center.

The only significant collection of Nairne manuscripts outside Great Britain is found in the Henry E. Huntington Library and Art Gallery, San Marino, California. Huntington Manuscripts 22269, Documents Relating to the Treason Trial of Thomas Nairne, consist of Nairne's petitions to Queen Anne and the Lords Proprietors and the petitions of other Carolinians in his behalf for release from the Charles Town jail. Pryce Hughes Letters Proposing a Welsh Colony in America, 1713, is a small collection in the South Caroliniana Library, University of South Carolina. These five letters, including one from Hughes to Nairne, document one aspect of his imperial vision—his fostering of Hughes' attempt to found "Annarea."

The political and diplomatic trail found in Nairne's *Journalls* is clearly marked by a large body of printed primary sources in English and French. Useful English materials are found in the multivolume *Calendar of State Papers, Colonial Series, America and West Indies*, edited by J.W. Fortescue, Cecil Headlam, and W. Noel Sainsbury, and published by the British government. Headlam edited *Volume 24* (London: HMSO, 1922) that contained pertinent British documents and a printed version of Nairne's memorial of July 10,1708. William S. Saunders' *Colonial Records of North Carolina*, 10 vols. (Raleigh: Josephus Daniels, 1890) is another source of BPRO materials relating to North and South Carolina. Alexander S. Salley's editions of S.C. public records, especially his 22 slim volumes of *Journals of the Commons House of Assembly*, are useful adjuncts to the manuscript journals at the S.C. Archives. The *Journal* for October 22,1707 to February 12,1707/8 (Columbia: S.C. Historical Commission, 1941) records the planning of Nairne's expedition and his political troubles with Governor Nathaniel Johnson. *The Journal of the Commissioners of the Indian Trade, September 20, 1710–August 29, 1718*, ed. William L. McDowell (Columbia: University of South Carolina Press, 1955) documents Indian-white relations throughout the Southeast.

French primary sources recount the intrusion of Nairne and Thomas Welch into territory France claimed as her own. Several French sources have been translated into English. Among them are Dunbar Rowland and A.G. Sanders, eds., *Mississippi Provincial Archives: French Dominion*, 5 vols. (Vols. 1–3, Jackson: Mississippi Department of Archives and History, 1927–1932; Vols. 4 and 5, ed. Patricia K. Galloway, Baton Rouge: Louisiana State University Press, 1984); John G. Shea's *Early Voyages Up and Down the Mississippi River, by Cavelier, St. Cosme, Le Sueur, Gravier, and Guignas* (Albany, N.Y.: Cramoisy Press, 1861); and *The Expedition of Don Diego de Peñalosa, Governor of New Mexico, from Santa Fe to the River Mischipi and Quivira in 1662* (New York: J.G. Shea, 1882) made available some accounts of the *coureurs*. Richebourg G. McWilliams has translated and edited André Penicault's 1699 narrative in *Fleur de Lys and Calumet, Being the Penicault Narrative of French Adventure in Louisiana* (Baton Rouge: Louisiana State University Press, 1953) and Pierre Le Moyne, Sieur d'Iberville's *Gulf Journals* (University: University of Alabama Press, 1981). These are good accounts of the interactions of French, Indians, and English on the lower Mississippi River. It is impossible to omit Pierre Margry's *Découvertes et Etablissements des Francais dans l'Ouest et dans le Sud de l'Amérique Septentrionale (1614–1754)*, 6 vols. (Paris: D. Jouaust, 1876–1886). Margry's work is badly marred by his obsession with Rene Robert, Cavelier de La Salle and, thanks to its inclusion in the Library of American Civilization microfiche collection (LAC 20730–35), it is perhaps too readily available to historians.

There are a few unofficial publications contemporaneous with the *Journalls*. The most important of them is Nairne's *A Letter from South-Carolina*, published in 1710. *A Letter from South-Carolina* is of signal importance as an account of social, political, and economic conditions in Carolina but says little about Southern Indians or British imperialism. It does not mention Nairne's expedition at all but these omissions ought not to be surprising. *A Letter* was primarily a promotional tract and any discussion of French and Spanish threats to British security would have been counterproductive. Also, Great Britain and France were still at war in 1710 and public knowledge of Nairne's journey might have compromised British strategy in the Southeast. Another pamphlet bears mention in conjunction with the *Journalls*. *Some Considerations on the Consequences of the French Settling Colonies on the Mississippi* (London: J. Roberts, 1720) articulated the imperial sentiments of Nairne, Richard Beresford, and John Barnwell. For a time Beresford was thought to have been its author but James Smith, a New Englander, is now known to have written it.

While there is a dearth of contemporaneous books and newspapers pertinent to the *Journalls*, there are other printed sources of value. The maps of Guillaume Delisle and Herman Moll are of signal importance to American cartography and Colonial Southern history. French and British soldiers with their Indian allies battled for hegemony in the Southeast during Queen Anne's War. European map makers engaged in a less sanguinary struggle to assert ownership of that region. Guillaume Delisle, royal cartographer of Louis XIV, and Herman

Moll, a Dutch resident of London, produced a series of maps during and after the War of Spanish Succession to assert their respective nations' claims to territory and Indian allegiance in the Southeast. Delisle published maps in 1703 and 1718 while Moll published in 1701, 1715, and 1720 (map 2 in text). In addition to chronicling British and French territorial aspirations Delisle and Moll preserved timely ethnohistorical and geographical information extant today in no other forms. Both cartographers interviewed and collected information directly from French and British explorers to improve the quality of their works. Jacques Bellin's *Remarques Sur la Carte de l'Amerique Septentrionale entre le 28e & le 72e degré de Latitude, avec une Description Géographique de ces Partes* (Paris: Didot, 1755) is a critical examination of the Delisle maps and others, and contain pertinent geographical information. Thomas Nairne's own "Map of South Carolina Shewing the Settlements of the English, French & Indian Nations from Charles Town to the River Missisipi" is important for geopolitical and ethnohistorical purposes. Its influence is readily seen in the printed maps of Delisle and Moll.

Two manuscript maps in the British Public Record Office help to explicate Nairne's *Journalls*. The so-called Richard Beresford map, *circa* 1715 (map 3 herein) and the John Barnwell map, *circa* 1722, contain a wealth of political, geographical, and ethnohistorical information. The handwriting of many notations on the Beresford map is similar to the handwriting of the copyist of Nairne's *Journalls* and is the only solid clue extant to the identity of the copyist. Beresford's map extends the western border of South Carolina to the Mobile River and the border of North Carolina to the confluence of the Ohio and Mississippi River. His political statement was obvious. The Beresford and Barnwell maps are in poor condition—particularly the latter. However, the Yale University Center for British Art, New Haven, Conn., recently acquired a manuscript map called the 'Hammerton State of the Barnwell Map." This version of the Barnwell map reveals many previously illegible notations concerning Indian village sites and events on the frontier. It is possible that William Hammerton, Secretary of the Province of South Carolina, might not only have made the Yale University copy but also have composed the Barnwell map in the first place.

Maps, like books, provide unique information but must be studied in context. William P. Cumming's *The Southeast in Early Maps* (revised ed., Chapel Hill: University of North Carolina Press, 1962) provides this context. Cumming reproduced many maps in this volume, including the Barnwell map, and composed a carto-bibliography of 450 Southern maps dating from 1544 to 1775. His introductory essay, carto-bibliography, and copious notes are authoritative.

Secondary works relating to the Southeast stem from one classic volume, Verner W. Crane's *The Southern Frontier, 1670–1732* (Durham, N.C.: Duke University Press, 1928). *The Southern Frontier* has been reprinted several times since 1928, but some of these editions omitted Crane's prodigious bibliography. The most recent edition, published in 1981 by W.W. Norton with an introduction by Peter H. Wood, restores intact a work of enduring value to a new generation of readers. Other monographs, some of Crane's era, are useful. Ella Lonn's *The*

Colonial Agents of the Southern Colonies (Chapel Hill: University of North Carolina Press, 1945); Henry Folmer's *Franco-Spanish Rivalry in North America* (Glendale, Ca.: A.H. Clark, 1953); and Mark Boyd and others, *Here They Once Stood: The Tragic End of the Apalachee Missions* (Gainesville: University of Florida Press, 1951) elucidate the imperial context of Nairne's *Journalls.* More recent works include M. Eugene Sirmans, *Colonial South Carolina, A Political History, 1663–1763* (Chapel Hill: University of North Carolina Press, 1966); David Corkran, *The Carolina Indian Frontier* (Columbia: University of South Carolina Press, 1970); Jay Higginbotham, *Old Mobile, Fort Louis de la Louisiane, 1702–1711* (Mobile: Museum of the City of Mobile, 1977); and Converse D. Clowse, *Economic Beginnings in Colonial South Carolina, 1670–1730* (Columbia: University of South Carolina Press, 1971).

Scholarly periodical literature and collections of essays contain pertinent work on Nairne and the Southeast. Charles W. Arnade's "The English Invasion of Florida, 1700–1706," *Florida Historical Quarterly* 41 (July 1962):29–37; Alexander Moore's "Thomas Nairne's 1708 Western Expedition: An Episode in the Anglo-French Competition for Empire," in *Proceedings of the Tenth Annual Meeting of the French Colonial Historical Society,* ed. Philip M. Boucher (Washington, D.C.: University Press of America, 1985), pp. 47–58; James D. Alsop's "Thomas Nairne and the 'Boston Gazette No. 216' of 1707," *Southern Studies* 22 (Summer 1983): 209–211; Philip M. Brown's "Early Indian Trade in the Development of South Carolina: Politics, Economics, and Social Mobility during the Proprietary Era," *South Carolina Historical Magazine* 76 (July 1977):118–128; and Peter H. Wood's "La Salle: Discovery of a Lost Explorer," *American Historical Review* 89 (April 1984):294–323, contribute to an understanding of Anglo-French relations in the region and the politics of early Carolina.

The collection of essays edited by Patricia K. Galloway, *La Salle and His Legacy. Frenchmen and Indians in the Lower Mississippi Valley* (Jackson: University Press of Mississippi, 1982) contains two essays in particular—John D. Stubbs, Jr., "The Chickasaw Contact with the La Salle Expedition in 1682" (pp. 41–48) and Galloway's "Henri de Tonti du Village des Chacta, 1702: The Beginnings of the French Alliance" (pp. 146–175)—that are of direct importance to Nairne's *Journalls.* In truth most of the fourteen essays are significant. They represent a new round of investigation of a topic—the French in the Mississippi Valley— that some might erroneously think exhausted. *La Salle and His Legacy* points out the continuing importance of traditional historical sources. The contributors' new approaches to old materials have yielded excellent results. The bibliography of this collection lists many of the titles mentioned in this essay and more.

The literature of ethnohistory, the second trail Nairne carved out in his *Journalls,* is large and of considerable age. The most notable book in English on Southeastern Indians is James Adair's *History of the American Indians; Particularly those Nations adjoining to the Mississippi, East and West Florida, Georgia, South and North Carolina and Virginia* (London: Edward and Charles Dilly, 1775). Adair's work is comparable in scope and significance to Robert Beverley's *History and Present State of Virginia* (London: R. Parker, 1705); Cadwallader Colden's

The History of the Five Nations Depending on the Province of New York (New York: William Bradford, 1727); and Joseph-François Lafitau's *Moeurs des Sauvages Amerquains Comparées aux Moeurs des Premier Temps* (Paris: Saugrain l'aine, 1724). Adair was a trader among the Chickasaws and recorded much information on the Muskhogean tribes gathered from first-hand informants and personal observation. However, Adair suffered from a serious bias. He fervently believed that American Indians were descendants of the Lost Tribes of Israel and spent a goodly portion of his *History* comparing Indian and Old Testament customs and rituals to prove his belief. Because of his comparative approach it is difficult to discern with any reliability what nation (Creek, Chickasaw, Choctaw, or Natchez) he discussed at any one time. For example, his discussion of Muskhogean busks is a *sine qua non* for ethnohistorians. But it is impossible to learn which tribes did or did not practice busks. Nairne flatly contradicts Adair in his *Journalls* on this point. Charles Hudson's "James Adair as Anthropologist," *Ethnohistory* 24 (Fall 1977):311-328; Wilcomb E. Washburn's "James Adair's 'Noble Savage,'" in *The Colonial Legacy: Volumes 3 and 4 in One, Historians of Man and Man's Nature*, ed. Lawrence Leder (New York: Harper and Row, 1973) pp. 91-120; and Robert M. Weir's "James Adair," in *Dictionary of Literary Biography, Volume 30, American Historians, 1607-1865*, ed. Clyde N. Wilson (Detroit: Gale Research, 1984), pp. 3-6, have subjected Adair's *History* to critical scrutiny. Although questions still linger about Adair's sources and his idiosyncratic notions, these writers have generally sustained his reliability.

The largest body of ethnohistorical writing on the Southeastern Indians is John R. Swanton's publications for the Smithsonian Institution. His "Social Organization and Social Usages of the Indians of the Creek Confederacy" and "Religious Beliefs and Medical Practices of the Creek Indians," in Smithsonian Institution Bureau of American Ethnology, *42nd Annual Report, 1924-1925* (Washington: GPO, 1928), pp. 23-472, 473-726; "Social and Religious Beliefs and Usages of the Chickasaw Indians," *BAE, 44th Annual Report, 1926-1927* (1928), pp. 169-273; and "Early History of the Creek Indians and their Neighbors," *BAE, Bulletin 73* (1922) are pertinent to Nairne's *Journalls*. Swanton's *magnum opus* is "Indians of the Southeastern United States," *BAE, Bulletin 137* (1946).

Other anthropological studies are John Witthoft's "Green Corn Ceremonialism in the Eastern Woodlands," in University of Michigan, *Occasional Publications from the Museum of Anthropology Number 13* (Ann Arbor: University of Michigan Press, 1949) and Fred Eggan's "Historical Changes in the Choctaw Kinship System," in *Essays in Social Anthropology and Ethnology* (Chicago: University of Chicago Department of Anthropology, 1975), pp. 71-90, first printed in 1937 in *American Anthropologist*. Arrell M. Gibson's "Chickasaw Ethnography: An Ethnohistorical Reconstruction," *Ethnohistory* 18 (Spring 1971):99-118; James H. Howard's "Some Chickasaw Fetishes," *Florida Anthropologist* 12 (June 1959):47-55; and William C. Sturtevant's "The Medicine Bundles and Busks of the Florida Seminole," *Florida Anthropologist* 7 (May 1954):31-41, are based on Adair's *History* and Swanton's work. The most recent synoptic work is Charles Hudson's *The Southeastern Indians* (Knoxville: University of Tennessee Press, 1976).

Hudson has culled most of the historical and anthropological literature and written a general text. Although he too depends upon Adair and Swanton he has also incorporated much recent scholarship. Hudson's extensive bibliography includes anthropological, archaeological, and historical sources.

Adair's *History* weighs heavily upon all anthropological literature of the Southeast. The absence of any other contemporaneous texts similar to Adair but independent of his work has kept the *History* an essential but not an ideal source. Swanton and Hudson have largely exhausted previously known ethnohistorical literature. Hence the significance of Nairne's *Journalls*. With anthropology at a temporary impasse, historical archaeology has taken up the challenge to illuminate the lives of Creeks, Chickasaws, and Choctaws. Recent investigations of the expeditions of Hernando De Soto, Cavelier de La Salle, Henri Tonti, and Nairne have made good contributions. Just as history and anthropology have a canon of classical texts so does historical archaeology. Jesse D. Jennings' "Chickasaw and Earlier Indian Cultures of Northeast Mississippi," *Journal of Mississippi History* 3 (July 1941):155–226, and James A. Ford's "Analysis of Indian Village Site Collections from Louisiana and Mississippi," Louisiana Geological Survey, *Anthropological Study Number Two* (New Orleans: Louisiana Department of Conservation, 1936) defined the dimensions of Mississippi and Louisiana historical archaeology. Richard A. Weinstein, "Some New Thoughts on the De Soto Expedition through Western Mississippi," *Mississippi Archaeology* 20 (1985):2–24; Gregory A. Waselkov, "Evolution of Deer Hunting in the Eastern Woodlands," *Mid-Continental Journal of Archaeology* 3 (Spring 1978):15–34; Richard L. Haan, "The 'Trade Do's Not Flourish as Formerly': The Ecological Origins of the Yamassee War," *Ethnohistory* 28 (Fall 1982):341–358; Don Martini, "The Search for Ackia," *Northeast Mississippi Historical Journal* 5 (November 1972):17–31; and James R. Atkinson, "The Ackia and Ougoula Tchetoka Chickasaw Village Locations in 1736 during the French-Chickasaw War," *Mississippi Archaeology* 20 (June 1985):53–72, have provided an archaeological basis upon which to evaluate Nairne's and Adair's assertions. Atkinson, Archaeologist at the National Park Service, Natchez Trace Parkway, Tupelo, Miss., is engaged in a comprehensive study of historical Chickasaw village sites in the Tupelo area.

Gregory A. Waselkov and Peter H. Wood are presently editing a collection of thirteen essays on Southeastern Indians. *Powhatan's Mantle*, forthcoming from the University of Nebraska Press, includes essays by Ian W. Brown on the calumet ceremony in the Southeast; Patricia Galloway on French-Choctaw relations; and Marvin Smith on aboriginal population movements. Peter Wood contributes an article on Indian demography and Waselkov one on Indian maps. Other contributors are Vernon J. Knight, Amy Bushnell, James Merrill, Helen Tanner, and Daniel H. Usner. *Powhatan's Mantle* assembles the work of scholars currently doing the best Southern archaeology and ethnohistory.

Throughout his *Journalls* Thomas Nairne made references to the literary and historical writings of European society. These references give modern readers a lens through which to view Nairne's mind at work as he observed and recorded the culture of the Southeastern Indians. Nairne's intellectual impedimenta un-questionably affected what he saw among the Indians and how he saw it. It is not surprising that most of his allusions—even the literary ones—are of a political character. A whig in politics, despite the charges against him of Jaco-bitism, and doubtless an adherent of the Glorious Revolution, he saw "whig-gish notions" in the consensual politics of the Ocheses and Chickasaws. Their society brought to mind the Republic of Plato and the Leveller principles of John Lilburne.

Gender relations, including polygyny and the relative sexual equality among the Muskhogeans, evoked a sensible and at times light-hearted response. Thanks to his familiarity with Cornelius Tacitus' *Germania* and Venerable Bede's *History of the Church of England*, he had no difficulty comprehending and appreciating Muskhogean matrilineal kinship systems. Similar systems had once existed among ancient German and Briton tribes. Evidence of female autonomy led Nairne to recall, half-seriously, John Milton's antifeminist *Samson Agonistes* (1671) and Trajan Boccalini's *I Ragguagli Di Parnasso: Or, Advertisements from Parnassus* (1674). These were the musings of a worldly-wise man remarkably free from prejudice and self-importance. He knew the Holy Bible well enough to quote chapter and verse when comparing Chickasaw and Hebrew rituals of friendship and discussed the Great Flood with the Chickasaws. In both these cases, however, Nairne utilized the Bible as a repository of historical and scientific knowledge, not of piety or inspiration. He probably held conventional Anglican religious beliefs but among the Indians his secular pragmatism prevailed.

Nairne was familiar with previous explorations in the Southeast. He knew of Hernando De Soto's 1540 *entrada* and the recent activities of Cavelier de La Salle and Henri de Tonti. However, the source of his knowledge is somewhat problematical. There were several accounts of De Soto's journeys available in English, Spanish, and Latin but his subsequent reference in the *Journalls* to the Inca Empire as arbiters of peace among smaller nations suggests that Nairne might have been familiar with the writings of Garcilaso de la Vega, El Inca. Garcilaso's *La Florida del Ynca* (1605) recounted De Soto's passage through the Southeast and his *Royal Commentaries of the Incas* (1688) was an important source in English of the notion of a Pax Incaia. The sources of Nairne's knowledge of La Salle, Tonti, and the enigmatic Dionisio de Penalosa are even more obscure. Louis Hennepin's *Description de la Louisiane* (Paris, 1683) and other works by Hennepin in English and French may have helped Nairne's understanding of the French activities in the region. Another possible work was *Dernieres Découvertes dans L'Amérique Septentrionale; Mises au jour par M. de Tonti, Gouverneur du Fort Saint Louis aux Islinois* (Paris, 1697). Because the French presence was so recent it is most likely that Nairne gathered intelligence first-hand from Indians or perhaps from the mysterious Jean Couture.

Index

LaVergne, TN USA
03 January 2011
210762LV00007B/85/A